THE FIRST AND THE FASTEST

THE FIRST AND THE FASTEST

COMPARING ROBIN KNOX-JOHNSTON AND ELLEN
MACARTHUR'S ROUND-THE-WORLD VOYAGES

NIGEL SHARP

The
History
Press

Front cover illustrations:

Top: 22 April 1969: Robin Knox-Johnston waving from his 32ft yacht *Suhaili* off Falmouth, England just before completing the world's first solo non-stop circumnavigation, having set out from Falmouth 312 days earlier. Even seasoned yachtsmen thought it would be an impossible feat, and for everyone else it was: of the nine starters in this *Sunday Times*-sponsored round-the-world race, Robin was the only finisher. (Credit: Bill Rowntree/PPL);

Bottom: 9 February 2005: Ellen Macarthur in Falmouth, soon after breaking the solo non-stop round-the-world record. She crossed the finishing line – between Ushant on the North coast of France and the Lizard on the Southwest coast of England – the night before, having completed the voyage in 71 days 14 hours 18 minutes and 33 seconds, over a day quicker than the time set by French sailor Francis Joyon a year earlier. (Credit: Phil Russell/PPL)

First published 2018

The History Press
The Mill, Brimscombe Port
Stroud, Gloucestershire, GL5 2QG
www.thehistorypress.co.uk

British Library Cataloguing in Publication Data.
A catalogue record for this book is available from the British Library.

ISBN 978 0 7509 8694 6

Typesetting and origination by The History Press
Printed and bound by CPI Group (UK) Ltd

Contents

With huge gratitude to Robin Knox-Johnston and Ellen MacArthur, for their contributions to this book, but, much more than that, for their epic voyages.

Foreword

I was 20 years old when Robin Knox-Johnston sailed into the record books. His solo non-stop circumnavigation remains the most significant small boat voyage from the past century and, as with thousands of others, had a major impact on my life.

A college student, I was captured by the whole adventure and avidly read every report on the *Sunday Times* Golden Globe Race. It was as much a race between Fleet Street's finest as it was on the water, with the *Sunday Mirror* (which sponsored Robin), *Sunday Express* and *News Chronicle* all vying to scoop *The Sunday Times* on their own story.

And there wasn't much news to go round. Knox-Johnston's radio was swamped by a wave early on in the Southern Ocean, and Frenchman Bernard Moitessier didn't even have one, relying instead on a catapult to fire nuggets of information to passing ships. But that didn't stop the Sunday papers from running double-page spreads each week and sending their correspondents on expensive wild goose chases in an effort to intercept these boats. In the weeks, even months, between valid reports and sightings, these correspondents simply interviewed their typewriters, pinpointed positions with the accuracy of a 6-pint darts player and swallowed whole the fraudulent position reports and speed record claims from Donald Crowhurst, who, instead of chasing the leaders round the globe, skulked around in the South Atlantic ready to 'slot back in' once the leaders had turned north after rounding Cape Horn.

These newspaper hacks were predicting that it would be a neck-and-neck finish from as far away as New Zealand, the last contact Knox-Johnston and Moitessier had with the outside world, and continued with this paper-selling pretence until the Frenchman fooled all the 'experts' by turning up in Table Bay, Cape Town and *Suhaili* was finally sighted by the oil tanker *Mobil Acme* two weeks before his finish.

In reality, Moitessier rounded Cape Horn nineteen days behind Knox-Johnston with neither knowing where the other was. Robin is a firm believer that the *Joshua* skipper, who had set out from Plymouth six weeks after *Suhaili* left Falmouth, knew in his heart that the race was 'lost' even before crossing the Date Line, and simply continued East after rounding Cape Horn to 'Save his soul' as Moitessier put it, because he was by then at one with the sea and didn't cherish the idea of returning to an increasingly commercial world.

The myth, still widely believed in France, is that Moitessier led Knox-Johnston around Cape Horn and would have won the race easily had he not been thinking on a higher plane.

But as readers, we lapped up whatever story would sell newspapers and thirsted for more. Knox-Johnston's triumphant return to Falmouth was the first live outside broadcast streamed by the BBC, the *Sunday Mirror* was the first to experiment with 'wiring' a photograph over the airwaves from out at sea, (to scoop *The Sunday Times* again), and thousands lined the waterfront to get a first sight of this new national hero.

Knox-Johnston's achievement was as significant then as Neil Armstrong's first steps on the Moon three months later. The voyage encouraged hundreds of thousands around the globe to jump in a boat and led me to take up sailing as a career. People with the fortitude, strength of character and sheer bloody determination to achieve such heights in life usually emerge just once a decade. Britain was lucky to have three emerge in one era: Francis Chichester, Alec Rose, Knox-Johnston – and Chay Blyth who, after dropping out of the *Sunday Times* race, returned to become the first to complete a solo non-stop circumnavigation the other way round.

It took another three decades before Britain could champion another superhero in the diminutive form of Ellen MacArthur, a 5ft 2in (1.57m) human dynamo. The challenge for her was very different to that faced by Knox-Johnston. Her 75ft (23m) trimaran was built for speed and equipped with every labour-saving device, and far from being alone with her thoughts for months at a time, as Robin had been, she had weather routers, mast, sail and boat technicians, and most of all a manager/mentor on call via satellite phone twenty-four hours a day.

This of course is the modern way, but her feat still required great fortitude and spirit. And by smashing the record by a day and a third, her achievement also had a major impact on reducing male chauvinism within the sport and led to a lot more young women taking part.

Barry Pickthall
Media Director, 2018 Golden Globe Race and Chairman
of the Yachting Journalists' Association.

Knox-Johnston's route

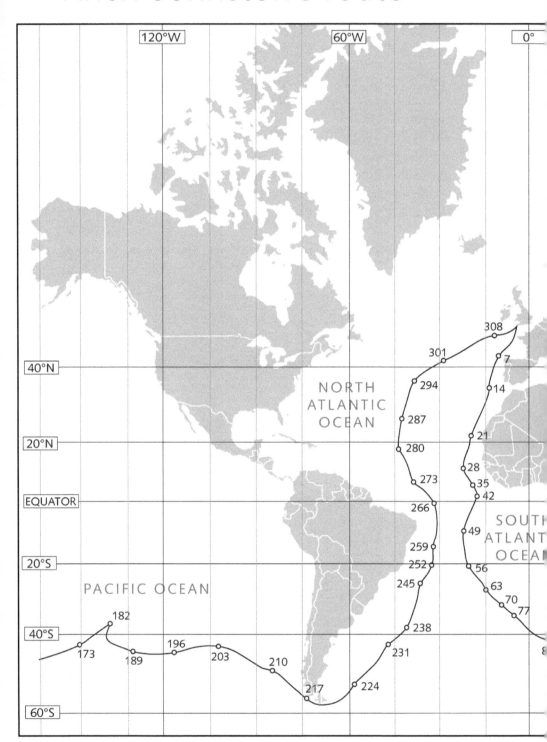

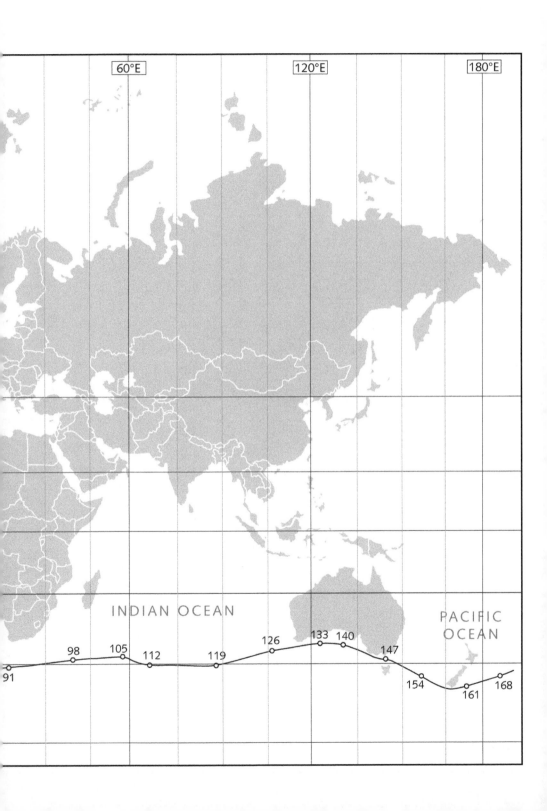

MacArthur's route

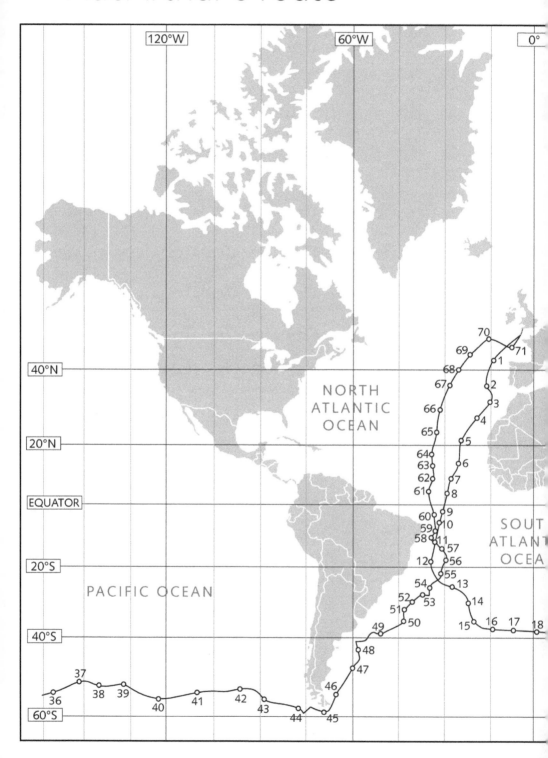

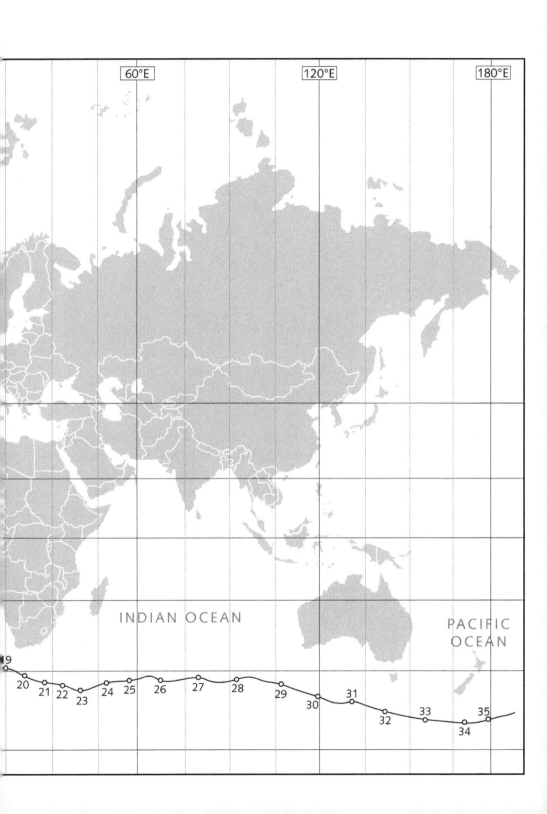

Introduction

Falmouth, Cornwall, is a town steeped in maritime history, but rarely can it have witnessed two more significant events than the arrival of two particular sailing boats: one in April 1969 and the other in February 2005. Although they were fundamentally different types of boats – one a 32ft 6in (9.9m) ketch with a 'wallowing trawler appearance' as she was later described in *The Sunday Times*, and the other a 75ft (22.9m) lightweight trimaran – they were inextricably linked by a common accomplishment: they had both been sailed from the same port single-handed and non-stop around the world and, in doing so, had reached hugely significant milestones in maritime history. The first was *Suhaili*, whose skipper Robin Knox-Johnston had left Falmouth 312 days earlier and had become the world's first non-stop solo circumnavigator; the second was Ellen MacArthur's *B&Q* which, in a little over seventy-one and a half days, had become the fastest.

Prior to Knox-Johnston's voyage, about thirty people had sailed single-handed around the world, but they had all stopped along the way, the majority of them numerous times. Of these, there were three particularly notable circumnavigators.

The very first was Joshua Slocum, who left Boston, USA in April 1895 in his 36ft 9in (11.2m) sloop *Spray*. His initial plan was to sail eastabout, but when he stopped in Gibraltar – with a view to then continuing through the Mediterranean Sea and the Suez Canal – he was advised by officers of Britain's Royal Navy who were stationed there that it would be dangerous to continue that way due to the threat of pirates. So he changed his mind and went westabout, and from Gibraltar he sailed across to South America, through the Straits of Magellan and eventually around the Cape of Good Hope and back to America. He arrived in Newport, Rhode Island – having converted *Spray* into a yawl by adding a mizzen mast along the way – in June 1898, having sailed 46,000 miles.

Vito Dumas was an Argentinian who, in June 1942, set off from Buenos Aires in his 32ft (9.76m) Colin Archer ketch *Lehg II* while most of the world was waging war. Four hundred and thirty-seven days later, he returned to the same port, having sailed around the world through the Southern Ocean, stopping just three times: in Cape Town, Wellington in New Zealand and Valparaiso, Chile. He was the first solo sailor to round Cape Horn.

Francis Chichester was a British adventurer who originally achieved fame though his solo flying exploits. In 1929 he flew a de Havilland Gipsy Moth biplane from England to Australia, taking forty-two days. Two years later he became the first person to fly solo from New Zealand to Australia, using the same aircraft but now fitted with floats so he could land and refuel at Norfolk Island and Lord Howe Island.

After the Second World War, he became interested in sailing, and in 1953 he bought a yacht called *Florence Edith* and changed her name to *Gipsy Moth II*. He raced her with increasing enthusiasm, and in 1959 he commissioned Robert Clark to design, and John Tyrrell of Arklow to build, a 40ft (12.2m) cutter, which he named *Gipsy Moth III*. The following year he was one of five competitors to compete in the very first single-handed transatlantic race, sponsored by the Observer newspaper and therefore known as the Observer Single-handed Transatlantic Race (or OSTAR). *Gipsy Moth III* won the race in a time of just over forty days, beating Blondie Haslar – who had done much to develop self-steering systems, which were fundamental to single-handed ocean racing – by eight days. Four years later, the OSTAR attracted fifteen competitors, but this time, although he improved his time by over ten days, Chichester's *Gipsy Moth III* was beaten into second place by the Frenchman Eric Tabarly in his custom-built 44ft (13.4m) ketch *Pen Duick II*. As a result of this, Tabarly was 'feted in his homeland,' *Yachting World* reported, 'and after a tumultuous welcome in Paris, General de Gaulle made him a Chevalier of the *Légion d'honneur.*'

Soon after completing the 1964 OSTAR, Chichester commissioned Illingworth and Primrose to design, and Camper and Nicholsons to build, a boat specifically for him to sail solo around the world, stopping just once. The result was the 53ft (16.1m) ketch *Gipsy Moth IV,* which Chichester famously came to despise, although it is generally considered that her flaws were the result of the unreasonable demands he made on her designers. On initial sea trials in the Solent, she heeled over alarmingly in a Force 6 gust. 'Here was a boat which would lay over on her beam ends in the flat surface of the Solent,' Chichester wrote, 'the thought of what she would do in the huge Southern Ocean put ice into my blood.' *Gipsy Moth* was then slipped so that 2,400lb (1,090kgs) of additional ballast could be added, but even then he described her as 'still horribly tender'. Once the voyage was under way he found more faults: she had a tendency to 'hobby horse' when sailing close hauled, whereby relatively small waves would reduce her speed significantly and, if she had four or five such waves in succession, she might even come to a standstill; he had trouble setting up the self-steering gear so that she would keep on course when close hauled; and finally she had a tendency to broach – 'as easily as a flick of the cane' – when sailing downwind in a big sea. He wrote after his circumnavigation:

> Now that I have finished I don't know what will become of *Gipsy Moth IV*. I only own the stern while my cousin owns two thirds. My part, I would sell any day. It would be better if about a third were sawn off. The boat was too big for me. *Gipsy Moth IV* has no sentimental value for me at all. She is cantankerous and difficult and needs a crew of three – a man to navigate, an elephant to move the tiller and a 3ft 6in chimpanzee with arms 8ft long to get about below and work some of the gear.

Nonetheless, she safely carried him around the world as he had planned. By the time he arrived back in Plymouth he was a national hero, and he was welcomed by a vast armada of small boats and a quarter of a million people on Plymouth Hoe. Soon afterwards he was knighted at Greenwich by Queen Elizabeth II with the same sword that her namesake had used to knight Francis Drake.

Chichester's declared target was to complete each of the two legs of his voyage – from Plymouth to Sydney and back again – in 100 days which, he estimated, was the average time it used to take the wool and grain clipper ships to sail the same route in the nineteenth century. In that respect he failed – he took 107 and 119 days – but the voyage was nonetheless ground-breaking. It was the first ever solo circumnavigation with only one stop; each leg of his voyage was more than twice the distance that he, or any other single-handed sailor, had ever sailed before; and it was also the fastest ever circumnavigation by any small vessel. He had paved the way for someone to go one better: to sail single-handed non-stop around the world.

The thought that he might attempt this feat first occurred to Robin Knox-Johnston in March 1967, when he was at his parents' home in Kent while on leave from his job as a merchant seaman. Chichester was still at sea and would not finish his voyage for a couple of months, and Knox-Johnston's father was reading a newspaper article about Eric Tabarly, who was planning to compete in the 1968 OSTAR in a new trimaran. Father and son began to speculate what other plans Tabarly might have, and whether these might include a non-stop solo circumnavigation. 'It's about all there is left to do,' said Knox-Johnston senior. This planted a seed of thought in his fiercely patriotic son's mind: it had to be a 'Brit' who would achieve this landmark voyage first.

In 2003, the record for sailing single-handed non-stop round the world was a little over ninety-three days. This had been set in a 60ft (18.3m) monohull by the Frenchman Michel Desjoyeaux when he won the 2000/01 Vendée Globe, the fourth edition of the race that was first held in 1989/90, and which starts and finishes in Les Sables-d'Olonne on France's west coast. Ellen MacArthur finished second in that race, just over a day behind Desjoyeaux, and two years later she made the decision to commission a trimaran with the express purpose of trying to break a number of records, including a circumnavigation. However, by the time her new boat was launched, her primary goal would be considerably more difficult: another Frenchman, Francis Joyon, had just completed the voyage in his own trimaran in a little less than seventy-three days. 'On that day the challenge before us got a whole lot bigger,' she later wrote.

Robin and Ellen

Robin Knox-Johnston

Robin Knox-Johnston was born in Putney, London on 17 March 1939, the eldest of four brothers. During the war, he and his family were bombed out of their flat near Liverpool and then moved to Heswall on the Dee Estuary, and it was there that his interest in boats took root. At the age of 4 he built a raft and carried it a mile to the sea, where it sank as soon as he stood on it. 'I had lost my first command,' he later wrote. His next craft – a 10ft (3.05m) canoe – came a decade later when he was a pupil at Berkhamsted School in Hertfordshire. He built her in his grandparents' attic, but she too sank, or at least initially, but she was later declared seaworthy when the family took her to Sussex for their summer holidays.

At the age of 17, Knox-Johnston was keen to join the Royal Navy. He duly sat the Civil Service Commission's exams, but didn't make the grade in all of the subjects. He later wrote that, at that time, he 'had difficulty in applying theory and experiments of the General Certificate syllabus to any practical problems that came my way.' So he decided to apply for the Merchant Navy instead, and on 4 February 1957 he joined the British India Steam Navigation Company's ship *Chindwara* as an Officer Cadet. He spent most of his apprenticeship on the *Chindwara* as she made her way backwards and forwards between London and various ports in East Africa, and in October 1960 he passed his Ministry of Transport Second Mate's Certificate exams. He then served on British India's *Dwarka* between Indian and Persian Gulf ports. In 1962 he married Sue, his childhood sweetheart, and they set up home in Bombay and subsequently had a daughter, Sara.

It was on his next ship, the *Dumra*, that he served with Peter Jordan, and the two of them decided to build a boat and sail it back to England with a view to selling it at a profit. The result was *Suhaili*, which was launched on 19 December 1964. Soon afterwards, Knox-Johnston returned to England to take his Master's Certificate and also to take up a new role as a Royal Naval Reserve Officer.

By this time, Jordan (and also Mike Ledingham, who had joined them in the *Suhaili* project) had made other plans, so when Knox-Johnston was ready to sail her home from India, he recruited his brother Chris and a Marconi radio officer called Heinz Fingerhut as crew. They set sail on 18 December 1965 – almost a year to the day after *Suhaili* had been launched – and, after calling at Muscat, Salala, Mombasa, Zanzibar, Dar-es-Salaam, Mtwara, Beira and Lourenco Marques, they arrived in Durban in April 1966. By now they had all run out of money, so they decided to stay in Durban and seek employment. After eight months' work – Knox-Johnston serving on merchant ships – and a further delay while they replaced *Suhaili*'s mainmast which had been broken in an accident, they set sail again. After calling at East London and Cape Town, they set off on the final non-stop leg back to England on 24 December. Seventy-seven days later, they arrived at Gravesend on the Thames.

Knox-Johnston then reported to British India that he was ready to resume his Merchant Navy career, but he was told that the ship on which he was due to serve as First Officer, the *Kenya*, wouldn't arrive in London for another month and so his leave would be extended. It was during that month that he had that fundamentally life-changing conversation with his father.

Ellen MacArthur

Ellen MacArthur was born in Derbyshire on 8 July 1976. Her parents were both teachers, and she had two brothers. Just as Knox-Johnston built his first vessel when he was 4, MacArthur first dreamt of being at sea at the same age. She first sailed when she was 8, on her Aunt Thea's 27ft (8.2m) boat *Cabaret* (a Diamond 27) at Burnham-on-Crouch, and it wasn't long before the family took regular holidays on the south coast with sailing at the top of the agenda. MacArthur later wrote that, whenever *Cabaret*'s sails were hoisted, she 'was riddled with a restless excitement'.

From then on, she began to save her dinner money – just keeping back 80p per day to buy beans and mash – and this allowed her to buy her first boat, a Blue Peter dinghy which she named *Threpn'y Bit*. She loved animals and had ambitions to be a vet but this plan reached a significant setback when she contracted glandular fever just before she was due to take her A-Levels. However, while she was laid up in bed she happened to watch a television programme about boats sailing around the world and this made a hugely significant impression on her. It was at that moment that she realised she would pursue a career in sailing.

She then began to teach sailing courses in Hull and she herself passed her Yachtmaster exams at the age of just 18, as a result of which she won the 1994 Young Sailor of the Year Award. When she was presented with this she had the opportunity of meeting her childhood hero Robin Knox-Johnston, with whom she found herself posing for photographs.

She then bought a Corribee 21 that she named *Iduna* and which, in 1995, she sailed around mainland Britain single-handed, anticlockwise via the Caledonian Canal. She set off from Hull on 1 June and in many of the thirty-nine ports she visited she made a point of meeting schoolchildren and local sailors at their yacht and sailing clubs Admittedly, she did 'race' for the last twenty-four hours to avoid arriving back in Hull on Friday 13 October: she got there the day before. In the process of the voyage she even managed to raise money for the RNLI. 'Everything about the journey fascinated me,' she wrote after she completed her voyage, 'and every decision, repair or manoeuvre was part of a huge puzzle that I was relishing the opportunity to solve.' *Iduna* was exhibited at the London Boat Show the following January and it was there that she met Mark Turner who was, at that time, the sales manager for the marine equipment company Spinlock.

During the course of 1996, MacArthur sailed offshore for the first time, crossing the Atlantic twice in Open 60s, two-handed both times. The first was a delivery trip from Boston, USA to France and then, almost as soon as they arrived, she flew to Canada so that she could race with Vittorio Malingri on his Open 60 *Anicaflash* in the Quebec to Saint-Malo race, a voyage on which they ran out of gas halfway, and of food two days before they finished.

In January 1997, she and Mark Turner formed a business partnership – which would soon become the company Offshore Challenges – while the two of them were planning to take part in the Mini Transat. This is a biennial single-handed race from Brest to Martinique via Tenerife, which is sailed in the 6.5 metre Mini class. MacArthur, sailing *Financial Dynamics*, was the only woman in the 51-boat fleet, and she finished twenty-sixth on the first leg and fifteenth overall, while Turner was fifth. After the race, Turner decided he would step back from competitive sailing so that he could manage both the company and MacArthur's subsequent sailing programme.

The next milestone in MacArthur's sailing career might have been the Around Alone – the four-yearly 'stopping' race around the world which was previously known as the BOC Challenge and would later be renamed the Velux 5-Oceans. The next edition was due to start in the latter part of 1998 from Charlestown, USA with stops in Cape Town, Auckland and Punta del Este before finishing back in Charlestown. MacArthur, however, was looking further forward, to the Vendée Globe, the non-stop round the world race, the next edition of which would start in Les Sables d'Olonne in November 2000. That was her real goal but she and Turner knew that she had to have the right preparation for it, and they decided that the Around Alone would detract from that. They thought she would be better off taking part in the French classic Route de Rhum – the four-yearly single-handed race from Saint-Malo to Guadeloupe – while watching the progress of the Around Alone competitors.

In June 1998 MacArthur took part in the two-handed Round Britain and Ireland Race with David Rowen in the Open 50 *Jeantex* and came first in class. She was then fortunate enough to come to a last-minute agreement to charter Pete Goss's Open 50 Aqua Quorum – in which he had competed in the previous Vendée Globe – to take part in the Route de Rhum.

The boat was renamed *Kingfisher* after the company whose high-street brands included Woolworths, Comet, B&Q, Castorama and Superdrug, and from whom she and Turner had managed to secure sponsorship. In a fleet of seventeen monohulls – most of them Open 60s – she finished fifth and was the first of the Open 50s. In recognition of this achievement she became the youngest ever winner of the Yachtsman of the Year award, and soon afterwards *Yachting World* described her as 'Britain's most single-minded 22-year-old'.

During the course of 1999, as part of her ongoing plan to learn as much as possible about racing Open 60s, MacArthur sailed with Frenchman Yves Parlier on his *Aquitaine Innovations*, first in the fully-crewed Round Europe race, and then in the two-handed biennial Transat Jacques Vabre from Le Havre to Cartagena, Colombia. She also took part in the Fastnet Race with Laurent Bourgnon in his 60ft (18.3m) trimaran *Primagaz*, campaigned a Laser 4000 dinghy with Olympic sailor Paul Brotherton to sharpen her racing skills, and received personal tuition regarding weather routing from meteorological expert Jean-Yves Bernot.

The boat in which MacArthur would do the Vendée Globe was designed by Merf Owen and Rob Humphreys, and built by Marten Yachts in New Zealand – the first Open 60 to be produced in that country. She was officially launched by Sir Peter Blake's wife Pippa – and christened *Kingfisher* – in Auckland on 18 February 2000, the eve of the America's Cup which Team New Zealand would successfully defend. 'Ellen climbed up to the first set of spreaders and popped open a bottle of champagne,' it was later reported in *Yachting World*. 'Firecrackers exploded and the boat and crowd were showered in streamers and confetti.'

At the time of the official launch, MacArthur had had a chance to sail her new *Kingfisher* just once. 'She handled brilliantly,' she said afterwards. But she soon got the opportunity to share a lot more sea miles with her. Part of the reason that a New Zealand company had been chosen as the builder was to give MacArthur experience of sailing in the Southern Ocean while bringing the boat back to Europe. For that stretch of the delivery she had a crew of three but after they got off the boat – in a cove called Caleta Martial, about 10 miles north of Cape Horn – she had the chance to sail her single-handed for the remaining 7,000 miles.

On 4 June 2000, just four months after *Kingfisher* was launched, MacArthur set off from Plymouth at the start of the Europe 1 New Man STAR single-handed race (the equivalent of Chichester's OSTAR) to Newport, Rhode Island – the first time she had raced an Open 60 solo.

In a fleet of nineteen IMOCA 60s, she became the first British winner of the race since 1968, a feat which *Yachting World* described as 'a colossal confidence boost for Ellen MacArthur'.

Five months later she was in Les Sables d'Olonne as the youngest ever entrant in the Vendée Globe, the start of which was delayed by four days due to a ferocious storm in the Bay of Biscay. The Frenchman Michel Desjoyeaux took the lead soon after reaching the Southern Ocean, at which point MacArthur was in fourth place, but when she rounded Cape Horn she had moved up to second, about 600 miles behind Desjoyeaux. On the way up the Atlantic she gained on him and before long the two boats were trading places. They were neck-and-neck at the equator but MacArthur's chances of winning were eventually scuppered when she hit a semi-submerged object – most likely a container – and had to slow down and make repairs. She eventually finished in second place, just a day behind Desjoyeaux but almost two days ahead of the third boat and over a week ahead of the fourth. She arrived back in Les Sables d'Olonne to a tumultuous welcome, which Andrew Bray, the editor of *Yachting World*, later described as 'quite the most incredible sight I have ever seen at any sailing event the world over, and that's in a career in sailing journalism of thirty years.'

MacArthur's Corribee *Iduna*, in which she had sailed around Britain less than six years earlier, had been refitted and shipped to Les Sables and put on show there. MacArthur was also taken aback by the welcome. 'I could not believe the crowds,' she said, 'It was the most amazing experience in my whole life, I thought they were cheering for someone standing behind me.' The image of her kissing the side of *Kingfisher* as soon as she stepped on to the pontoon has become a particularly iconic moment in MacArthur's sailing history. 'The best thing in the race was crossing the finishing line, the hardest was leaving my boat,' she explained. Soon afterwards she won the Yachtsman of the Year award for the second time.

Desjoyeaux was now the fastest ever solo circumnavigator and MacArthur the second. But soon after she finished the Vendée, she and Turner formulated a five-year plan that included an attempt at this solo non-stop round the world record. 'Since being in the Southern Ocean in the Vendée,' she said, 'I'd been both enchanted by and drawn to its seductive beauty, and I knew I had to return there.' However, she knew that she would need to attempt such a record in a multihull and she also knew that she had practically no multihull experience – that was something that she would start to address later in the year.

Her next race on *Kingfisher* was as co-skipper (with Nick Maloney, another normally-solo sailor supported by Ocean Challenges) in the fully-crewed EDS Atlantic Challenge, a five-leg race which started from Saint-Malo in July and involved two Atlantic crossings. *Kingfisher* won three of the five legs, and overall victory.

At the end of 2001, MacArthur again took part in the Transat Jacques Vabre two-handed race – again starting from Le Havre but this time finishing in Salvador de Bahia in Brazil, making it the first transatlantic race to cross the equator – with her good friend Alain Gautier on his ORMA 60 trimaran *Foncia*. They finished second in a fleet of fourteen boats.

At the London Boat Show in January 2002, MacArthur announced that she intended to challenge for the Jules Verne Trophy, and would be looking for a suitable boat and recruiting a crew to do so. This competition had been inaugurated in 1991 to see if any fully-crewed boat could sail around the world – starting and finishing on a line between the Lizard Point and Ushant – in under eighty days. The first boat to win the trophy was the catamaran *Commodore Explorer*, which completed her voyage in a little more than 79 days and 6 hours in 1993. At the time that MacArthur made her announcement, the record stood at 71 days and 14 hours – achieved by Oliver de Kersausen's trimaran *Sport Elec* – but, shortly afterwards, Bruno Peyron's catamaran *Orange* reduced it still further to 64 days and 8 hours. 'The bar for us was undoubtedly raised higher,' said MacArthur. However, it soon became apparent that *Orange* herself was available and so MacArthur's sponsors, Kingfisher PLC, bought the boat, thus solving one of the major issues. However, this giant catamaran already need a serious refit, and matters got worse when, before MacArthur's team was able to take her over, she was dismasted while sailing in the Mediterranean. Luckily, a spare tube section was readily available, although there was a fair amount of work involved to complete, rig and step it, and this work wasn't completed until mid-December.

Meanwhile, MacArthur was racing her Open 60 *Kingfisher* for the last time, in the Route de Rhum. Once again, she won her class but this time she did so two days ahead of the record time and even finished before any of the multihull class, which had been decimated by appalling weather. It was the first time that a monohull had crossed the finish line first in the 24-year history of the Route de Rhum, which *Yachting World* described as 'the race that confirmed her ascendancy as Britain's finest offshore sailor'.

For her Jules Verne attempt, MacArthur had thirteen crew, four of whom knew *Orange* well as they had sailed on her with Peyron when breaking the record in 2002. This was a far cry from the single-handed and two-handed sailing that had dominated her sailing career to date, and she realised that much of it was a new experience for her.

With *Orange* re-named *Kingfisher II*, she moved from Cowes, where the refit work had taken place, to Lorient, which would allow easy access to the Atlantic during the short time available after the new rig was stepped. On 15 January 2003, the crew went on standby, awaiting news from their shore-based weather router that the conditions would be good to start. Just over a week later they were called back to the boat and, on 27 January, they set sail. On the way to the start line, around 100 miles away, they noticed that there was some damage to the mast track and so they headed to Plymouth to fix it. After a quick repair, they set off again and crossed the start line in gusts of 60 knots.

Not only would MacArthur and her crew be pacing themselves against *Orange's* record, but also against another boat – the trimaran *Geronimo*, in which Oliver de Kersausen was trying to reclaim the record – which had started before them and was now heading into the Indian Ocean.

Just over three weeks later, *Kingfisher II* was, herself, about halfway across the Indian Ocean. After a relatively slow start, things had been going better for her: she had just overtaken *Orange's* record pace and news had come through that *Geronimo* – which had been two days ahead of the record – was just past Cape Horn and beginning to slow. But, just before dawn on 22 February, when they were about 100 miles past the Kerguelen Islands, disaster struck. MacArthur was at the chart table at the time, discussing the weather with her shore-based weather router on the sat-phone, when she was 'jolted forwards' just as she heard a 'gut wrenching, ear-piercing, crunching and snapping sound'. At first she thought that *Kingfisher II* had hit an iceberg but that was not the case: the mast had snapped.

Within an hour, the fourteen crew managed to cut the rig free before it had a chance to seriously damage the hull, and the next day the boom and the surviving 10m section of the mast was used to build a jury rig. Freemantle, for which they now headed, was 2,200 miles away, and crew member Andrew

Preece later wrote that 'it wasn't long before the motion of the boat as it rocked and wracked along at 5 knots became painful and depressing and we all withdrew into our personal shells.'

Geronimo, incidentally, completed her circumnavigation but in too slow a time, but the following year de Kersausen – on his fourth attempt in this boat and his eighth in total – succeeded in regaining the Jules Verne trophy.

Despite the fact that her Jules Verne attempt had ended in failure, MacArthur took away from it a very positive attitude as she was now confident that it was possible to sail a multihull in the Southern Ocean and that it was worth having a go at the solo record. 'As soon as she flew home from Australia, she began to attend a series of meetings to discuss the design details of her new trimaran, and four weeks later construction began at Boatspeed in Sydney.

Meanwhile she set off on another ill-fated multihull voyage. In May, she was back on board Gautier's *Foncia*, this time with three other crew, to take part in the Challenge Mondial Assistance race starting from Cherbourg and bound for Rimini on the east coast of Italy. However, on the second morning, while in fourth place and sailing at around 23 knots under gennaker and full mainsail in about 25 knots of wind and glorious sunshine, the leeward rudder hit an unidentified semi-submerged object. *Foncia* immediately bore away dramatically and capsized.

Thankfully it was soon established that all the crew were safe – and, as it happens, three of them were already wearing survival suits – but they then spent twenty-four hours in the upturned hull which MacArthur later described as 'cold and sobering', with each of them taking it in turns to keep watch outside, while awaiting rescue. At the time *Foncia* was about 50 miles west of Lisbon and, when the salvage tug arrived, she was towed at about 3 knots – still upside down – to Cascais.

Undeterred, MacArthur continued her multihull training by taking part in the Archipelago Raid in Sweden in a Formula 8 catamaran with Nick Maloney. This is a gruelling race that would have taken six days and five nights, but the pair had to retire after MacArthur injured her leg.

At the end of the year, she was back on board the salvaged *Foncia* with Gautier for another attempt at the Transat Jacque Vabre in the hope of going one better than their 2001 position. This time, however, they were out of luck: after they broke the main halyard and tore the staysail, they put in to

Porto Santo in Madeira for repairs and, after re-joining the race, they could only manage ninth place.

But now she was able to concentrate on her new trimaran, *B&Q*, or *Mobi* to use the nickname that MacArthur gave her. After initial sea trials in Sydney, MacArthur and a crew took her to Auckland, from where they began six weeks of intensive sailing which served as both further sea trials for the boat and training for MacArthur.

B&Q then left Auckland and headed east towards Cape Horn, bound for the Falkland Islands with MacArthur, Turner and Loick Gallon, with whom she had sailed on *Foncia*, on board. During the course of the voyage they subjected the boat to increasingly stringent tests, and occasionally Turner and Gallon would take a back seat while MacArthur sailed singlehanded to ensure that everything worked for her and to ascertain what modifications might be needed.

As they arrived in the Falklands, two RAF Tornados put on a spectacular air display to welcome them. Although there was work to do on the boat during their five days there, they also had the opportunity for some relaxation, and to enjoy the warm hospitality of the local residents and the British military personnel stationed there. Then it was time for *B&Q* to set sail again and head north, but this time with just MacArthur on board.

Forty-four days after leaving Auckland, *B&Q* arrived in Newport, Rhode Island, USA, where she would be on standby waiting for suitable weather for a solo transatlantic record attempt. MacArthur managed a short visit back to the UK but *B&Q* remained in the USA for two months while the weather refused to cooperate. Eventually it was decided to abandon this attempt and bring the boat back to Europe with a crew of four, and so she was loaded with the necessary stores – including a few extraneous items such as a Wendy house that Gallon had made for his daughter. They were about to depart when they had a call from Commanders' Weather – the shore-based weather routers that MacArthur would also use for her circumnavigation – to say that the weather looked favourable to start a record attempt the following day. The Wendy house and most of the stores were hurriedly unloaded and then MacArthur set off. On the second night, *B&Q* met some horrendous seas and heeled over to an angle of 35 or 45 degrees, MacArthur estimated, and she thought, for a moment, that the boat would capsize.

They survived, however, but, after a fast passage in which MacArthur managed about fourteen hours sleep in seven days, she missed the 10-year-old record by a heartbreaking seventy-five minutes.

The Golden Globe – the Conception

It was probably John Ridgway who took the first steps towards embarking on a solo non-stop circumnavigation. He had already achieved fame in 1966 after spending ninety-two days rowing across the Atlantic in the 20ft (6.1m) *English Rose III* with fellow SAS soldier Chay Blyth. Ridgway had little sailing experience – and none of it single-handed – and his initial intention was to compete in the 1968 OSTAR and then start his circumnavigation the following year. In June 1967 he met David Sanders, the managing director of Westerly Marine, to discuss the possibility of doing this in one of his company's production boats. Sanders agreed to lend him a Westerly 30. At that time, Westerly Marine was advertising their 'magnificent 30' as 'the spirit of a racer … she's a fast twin-keel sloop with a real sailing hull' and 'wonderful for family cruising'. The company's range of boats was described as having 'advanced hull designs, beautiful cabins and handsome finishes.' At the time, the price of a Westerly 30 was £4,250, excluding the engine.

In late July, Ridgway sailed the borrowed Westerly 30 from Plymouth, around the Fastnet Rock and back again. This not only served as a qualifying passage for the OSTAR, but also convinced him that this type of boat would serve his purposes well, and so he ordered one for delivery the following year. She would be called *English Rose IV*.

Towards the end of the year, the Frenchman Bernard Moitessier also began to consider a circumnavigation. He already had a suitable boat – the 53ft (16.1m) *Joshua* (named after Slocum) in which he and his wife Francoise had sailed from Marseilles through the Panama Canal to Tahiti, and back again via Cape Horn. The return voyage included a non-stop leg of 14,216 miles from Tahiti to Alicante where they arrived in the spring of 1966, which was longer than any yacht had sailed at that time. By now he was a national hero in France. But he soon became very depressed, not least because he felt that the book he wrote about his voyage was produced too quickly, and he later began to believe that his salvation would come with a more ambitious voyage and another book.

Before the end of 1967, a third contender began to make plans. Bill King had been a submarine commander during the Second World War, and was said to be the only man to command a British submarine on both the first and the last days of the war. Inspired by Chichester's voyage, he commissioned Angus Primrose to design, and Souter's of Cowes, Isle of Wight, to build, a new 42ft (12.8m) boat. She would be called *Galway Blazer II* and her rig – partly designed by King's friend Blondie Haslar – was that of an unstayed junk-rigged schooner. The cost of the build was partly sponsored by the *Daily Express* and the *Sunday Express* newspapers.

At the London Boat Show in January 1968, news got out regarding two of these three. Firstly, there were strong rumours that Moitessier was preparing for another significant voyage and it didn't take much for anyone to realise what this might be; and then the *Daily Express* took it upon itself to publish details of *Galway Blazer*, even though King had wanted to keep his plans secret. This news prompted Ridgway to forget about the OSTAR and bring his circumnavigation plans forward by a year, and to leave as early in the summer as practical before King's inevitably faster boat would be launched. Not only did Ridgway visit the Boat Show (where he probably took the opportunity to discuss details of his new boat with Westerly) but so did his former rowing partner Blyth, as he too was considering a similar production boat – but from another company – for a circumnavigation of his own. Bizarrely, however, neither knew of the other's plans at that time.

By early February, Robin Knox-Johnston – who had considered commissioning a new boat, but by now had decided to take *Suhaili* – was making plans to set sail in early June. He was now aware of Ridgway's and King's intentions and he too was conscious of the potential speed of *Galway Blazer II* and so hoped to make an early start. However, he was keen to keep his plans secret for as long as possible – in fact for a time he claimed to be preparing for the 1968 OSTAR – and luckily his sponsors, the *Sunday Mirror*, agreed to do so.

Newspaper sponsorship for such ventures was clearly prevalent at that time. *The Sunday Times* had sponsored Francis Chichester's voyage and, although it had been initially reluctant to do so, it found that it paid huge dividends when he returned to his hero's welcome, and so was keen to continue its support of solo circumnavigators. Initially the newspaper thought it would sponsor another individual boat or sailor, and reporter Murray Sayle was tasked with considering the options.

As it happens, Knox-Johnston had already approached them about sponsorship. Sayle, however, thought he would have no chance of winning but that 'Tahiti' Bill Howell, an Australian dentist based in London, would be a much better bet. Howell had finished sixth in the 1964 OSTAR in his 30ft (9.1m) monohull *Stardrift*, and was reputed to have 20,000 miles of single-handed sailing experience under his belt. He now had a 40ft (12.2m) catamaran called *Golden Cockerel* that he intended to enter for the 1968 OSTAR and, as soon as he crossed the finish line, literally turn left and set off around the world. The OSTAR, he later said, would be 'only a bit of a prelude'.

But then the newspaper decided that sponsoring an individual sailor would, from a public perception point of view, be too similar to the Chichester experience, even if this next voyage was non-stop. It was then that Sayle, and his head of department Ron Hall, came up with a better idea: to sponsor a single-handed non-stop round-the-world race. In doing so they realised that, because various people already had their own plans that they would be reluctant to change, a conventional start – at a specific time and place – was not an option, as the official race might be a non-event. So they came up with a simple set of rules which they hoped would suit everyone.

They decided to offer two prizes: the Golden Globe trophy for the first solo circumnavigator, and £5,000 for the fastest during the coming 1968/69 'season'. The former would provide motivation for the smaller, slower boats as long as they were ready to make an early start; while the latter would suit those boats that would be unable to start early, but which were faster. The two-prize idea largely came about because the two journalists had different views on which would be the more significant achievement: Sayle thought it would be the first non-stop solo circumnavigation, Hall thought it would be the fastest.

A great deal of flexibility was allowed with regard to starting times and ports. Competitors could start at any time between 1 June and 31 October; from a port north of latitude 40-degrees North to be eligible for the Golden Globe trophy; and from a port on the British mainland for the cash prize. Each boat must, however, return to the same port from which it had started, having rounded the three great capes: Good Hope, Leeuwin and Horn.

The Sunday Times announced its race on 17 March 1968 with the headline: 'Round-the-world alone and non-stop: the toughest sailing race'. The article led with a quote from Sir Francis Chichester, who said that sailing around the world alone and non-stop was the 'Everest of the sea' and had never been successfully attempted. He thought that the feat, though possible, would be 'appallingly difficult'.

The five-month starting window was clearly to allow the maximum entry – including anyone, like Howell, who wanted to compete in the OSTAR first – but the newspaper had other reasons for limiting it to that period: although the risks would be significant throughout the whole voyage, it was likely that the most dangerous parts would be the Southern Indian Ocean (where both Francis Chichester and Vito Dumas had experienced the worst weather) and Cape Horn, and that the best times to be in those areas would be early summer and late summer respectively. This meant that it would be best to leave British shores in July or August.

The 40-degree North latitude port stipulation for the Golden Globe trophy was clearly to allow Moitessier – who at that time was determined to start from his home port of Toulon in the south of France – to compete.

The other rules were very simple. Each circumnavigation had to be completed without outside physical assistance which essentially meant that no fuel, food, water or equipment could be taken on board after the start; there were no restrictions on the design or build of competing yachts;

and there was no need for any formal entry as long as the departure was witnessed by a national newspaper. This last rule was largely to prevent any embarrassment that might come about if a competitor who hadn't entered became the first to complete the voyage. Not only would he not be associated with *The Sunday Times*, but there was a good chance he might be sponsored by another newspaper.

The Sunday Times was concerned that it might be accused of irresponsibility by sponsoring such a race without asking competitors to show, in any formal way, that they were equipped to deal with the huge potential risks. The newspaper made it clear that it had no wish to encourage suicide attempts, and that if competitors hoped to complete the voyage successfully they must have a high level of seamanship and properly equipped boats. Furthermore, the race was given credibility by Sir Francis Chichester's appointment as the chairman of a yet-to-be-announced internationally-recognised committee of judges who would ensure fair play in the spirit of single-handed seamanship.

The article said that four men were already known to be making preparations, and of these, two – King and Moitessier – had already publicly stated that they would be starting in August. Chichester himself expressed concern about the hazards that lay ahead. He thought that some of the potential competitors didn't know what they were letting themselves in for, and that it would be remarkable if any of them achieved a successful circumnavigation. By comparison, he thought, 'the Atlantic is about on the level of a canoe trip across the Serpentine.' The article finished on a positive note, comparing a non-stop solo circumnavigation with other 'ultimate' challenges such as the four-minute mile and the ascent of Everest, both of which had been successfully achieved during the previous fifteen years.

News of Moitessier's intentions reinforced Knox-Johnston's resolve to leave as early as possible – in fact as soon after 1 June as he could be ready – as he calculated that *Joshua* would be able to complete the voyage about a month quicker than the much smaller *Suhaili*. As it happened, at that time neither Moitessier nor King were interested in taking part in a race: each just wanted to complete a solo circumnavigation independently. However, as there was no requirement to make an official entry, neither could avoid being part of it.

A week after announcing the race, *The Sunday Times* reported that, subject to securing sponsorship, there would be two new competitors. One of these was Geoff Chaffey who had competed in the 1964 OSTAR in his

31ft (9.4m) cutter *Ericht II*, finishing in twelfth place after more than sixty days. In the event his interest would come to nothing but the other potential new competitor was Donald Crowhurst who was said to have extensive single-handed experience in his cutter *Pot of Gold* and was the manufacturer of the Navicator radio direction finder. On the day that Chichester arrived back in Plymouth, Crowhurst had been sailing in the Bristol Channel with a friend, to whom he said that he wanted to sail around the world non-stop and that the idea had first occurred to him four years previously. He would come to play a hugely controversial part in the Golden Globe race.

That issue of the newspaper also announced the composition of Chichester's panel of judges: Blondie Haslar (who later resigned as he recognised that he was too closely associated with Bill King), Michael Richey (the executive director of the Institute of Navigation who would be competing in the 1968 OSTAR), Alain Gliksman (the editor of the French magazine *Neptune Nautisme* and another OSTAR entry) and CD Hamilton (the editor-in-chief of Times Newspapers and a keen yachtsman). The new judges took the opportunity to warn competitors that they must be mentally and physically fit, have well-found vessels with adequate equipment and with back-up systems.

The Sunday Times announced Knox-Johnston's entry on 7 April and considered that he might be the least-experienced single-handed sailor in the race. However, the article also referred to *Suhaili's* impressive performance during her voyage back from India, while Knox-Johnston himself was reported as saying that she might not be the fastest entry, but that she would get him around the world safely.

Moitessier was reported to be still preparing for an August departure from Toulon which would make him eligible for the Golden Globe trophy but not the cash prize. But *The Sunday Times* was very keen that someone with his profile should be seen as a proper competitor, and so Murry Sayle travelled to Toulon in an attempt to persuade him to start from a British port. Sayle found him taking a break from his busy preparations in a dockside café, but was completely taken aback by his absolute refusal to have anything to do with the *Sunday Times* race. 'I was incensed at *The Sunday Times*, which had decided to organise a solo non-stop race around the world,' Moitessier later wrote. However, the two met again a couple of days later, and Sayle was equally taken aback to find that Moitessier had had a complete change of mind and had decided to start from Plymouth after all, apparently, it is said, 'on the whimsical ground that he liked Sayle's face' (Nicholas Tomlin and Ron Hall, *The Strange Voyage of Donald Crowhurst*). Moitessier further wrote that he was 'hoping to be able to carry off one or even both of the prizes, the good Lord willing, without risking our freedom, since the rules did not specify that we had to say "Thank you".'

At the end of April, it was revealed that Crowhurst was hoping to enter the race in *Gipsy Moth IV*. She was now owned by Lord Dulverton, who had largely financed her build and subsequently purchased Chichester's share, and there were plans to put her on permanent display alongside the *Cutty Sark* at Greenwich. Crowhurst had actually first contacted the Town Clerk at Greenwich about the matter in January: 'I believe there is not a single hazard attendant on my proposal that I have not considered,' he had written in this first letter, which was passed on to the Cutty Sark Society.

Crowhurst repeatedly argued that *Gipsy Moth IV* would be the most suitable boat for the Golden Globe, despite the fact that he had read all the derogatory remarks Chichester had written about her. He was offering a charter fee of £5,000 plus any prize money he might win, which would have been an attractive offer bearing in mind that the joint appeal by the Cutty Sark Society and the Mayor of Greenwich to raise the £17,000 needed to create the exhibition had met with a disappointing response. While Frank Carr of the Cutty Sark Society was said to be sympathetic to Crowhurst's proposal he also pointed out that 'it would be terrible if, by some misfortune, there were no boat to berth at the end of the race'. Despite Crowhurst's persistence over many months and public support from two sailing magazines, nothing came of his offer.

In the April issue of *Yachting World*, the editor Bernard Hayman also reported on *Gipsy Moth's* move to Greenwich but was somewhat negative about the *Sunday Times* race.

> Presumably, as soon as this [non-stop solo circumnavigation] has been achieved or, even before it's been achieved, some other industrial giant will dream up an even wilder scheme. How about a circumnavigation without going on deck; or even one sailing backwards?

The following month, *Yachting Monthly's* correspondent Argus wrote a piece which started: 'I must confess to being undecided whether a round-the-world non-stop single-handed race is a good thing.' He thought that competitors should be allowed to put in to port to enable them to make seamanlike decisions and that a non-stop race was a 'stunt in which chance will be the most potent factor'. But he conceded that 'one must be careful before decrying new ideas' while referring to the controversy surrounding the first Fastnet race in 1925 and the first OSTAR in 1960. He concluded:

> As planned, the race resembles one in which competitors are lined up beside a wide road on a blind corner where the traffic density is high, and told to get to the other side as quickly as possible without using the islands in the middle.

On 19 May, with the first opportunity for starting the race less than a fortnight away, John Ridgway's intentions became news when *The Sunday Times* announced the Atlantic rower's intention to take part in the race. However, unlike the other four known competitors who would be starting from the British mainland, Ridgway had decided to start from the Island of Inishmore in Galway Bay, Ireland. It was there that, on 3 September 1966, he and Blyth had made their landfall at the end of their epic Atlantic row and he had such an emotional attachment to the place that he decided to start his circumnavigation from there, even though it would mean he was ineligible for the £5,000 prize cash prize. But it was reported that the judges were considering whether to stretch the rules of the race so as to include him and, sure enough, they soon did so. Ridgway – who was being sponsored by the *People* newspaper – was, at that time, in a boatyard in Bursledon, Hampshire, making final preparations to *English Rose IV* before setting sail for Inishmore.

Meanwhile Moitessier was painting *Joshua*'s hull in Toulon, from where he hoped to sail for Plymouth on 1 June, and King's *Galway Blazer II* had now left her builder's yard and was at a Thames-side dock where he was preparing her for his voyage. But the big news was that Chay Blyth was now reported as being very interested in competing if he could find a sponsor and someone to lend him a boat.

A week later *The Sunday Times* reported that Bill Howell still intended to circumnavigate after he had completed the OSTAR which was to start the following Saturday, 1 June. There was also a first mention of another French entry, Loick Fougeron. He had a 4-year-old 29ft (8.8m) steel gaff cutter called *Captain Browne* which he was, at that time, sailing from Belgium (where he had bought her) to Casablanca (where he lived) to make the necessary alterations for the trip. He would then sail her to Falmouth in mid June with a view to starting the Golden Globe race from there.

On 1 June, Ridgway set sail from Inishmore. The night before, he and his wife Marie-Christine had attended a dance in the parish hall arranged in their honour by the locals who held him in great esteem, a feeling that was clearly mutual. 'I feel a real affinity for the islanders who live so closely with the sea,' he said, 'good people, who know what suffering is.' Ridgway said that he was pleased that the rules had been changed to allow him to start there – another reason for which, he said, apart from the emotional ties, was that he would have 'hated the kind of fuss there would have been if I'd sailed from Portsmouth where the boat was built' – and still qualify for the cash prize. *English Rose IV* was towed out of the harbour by the same lifeboat that had towed *English Rose III* in almost two years earlier, but soon afterwards she collided with a fishing boat from which Marie-Christine and other well-wishers were seeing him off, resulting in some inconsequential damage to the timber rubbing strake.

On the same day, thirty-five boats crossed the OSTAR start line in Plymouth, albeit very slowly as there was very little wind. *The Sunday Times* reported that, for Howell and his catamaran *Golden Cockerel*, it would be the beginning of a very long voyage. His latest plan, in order to comply with the Golden Globe rules, was that, as soon as he finished the OSTAR, he would sail back to Britain with a *Sunday Times* reporter crewing for him, and would then immediately set off single-handed round the world.

Just over a week later, on 8 June, Blyth set sail from Hamble. This may seem astonishing given that it had only been three weeks since he was reported as being 'very interested' in competing if he could find a boat and a sponsor. However, it had actually been several months earlier that his boat – a Kingfisher 30 bilge keeler called *Dytiscus III* – had been lent to him by the Westfield Engineering Company who built the Kingfisher range of boats in Poole, Dorset, and so clearly his attempts at keeping his plans secret had been very effective. Westfield Engineering advertised 'this very popular luxurious Bermudian yacht for cruising and racing' as having 'unrivalled comfort and performance ... She is fast, roomy and possesses excellent sea-going qualities'. The advertised cost was £3,950 'including sails'.

But at that time Blyth had practically no sailing experience of any kind: in fact, it is thought that he may have only sailed about 6 miles in his life. All too aware of this, he arranged for two other boats, both sailed by friends, to help him by leaving the Hamble with him: one would take the lead so that Blyth could copy his actions, and the other would trail behind and try to keep other craft away from him. They would only stay with him until they passed the Needles and entered the English Channel, however. From there on he was very much on his own.

The third boat to set sail – from Falmouth on 14 June – was *Suhaili*. Knox-Johnston had been preparing his boat in Surrey Docks on the Thames, close to his parents' home, and he set off from there on 3 June with a crew of three, including a reporter, Bruce Maxwell, and a photographer, Bill Rowntree, both from the *Sunday Mirror*. After stopping in Newhaven on the way, they arrived in Falmouth on 9 June. Five days later, Knox-Johnston left Falmouth alone on *Suhaili* at the beginning of his historic voyage.

A week later, *The Sunday Times* announced two new entries: Yves Wallerand of St Tropez – who planned to sail his La Gitana to Plymouth, from where he would start his circumnavigation, in early August – and Nigel Tetley. Tetley was a Lieutenant Commander in the Royal Navy from which he was due to retire the following February. He and his wife Eve lived in Plymouth on board their 40ft (12.2m) Piver-designed Victress-class trimaran *Victress* on which they had cruised extensively around Europe. He had decided he wanted to do the race almost as soon as it was announced in March and had hoped to secure a sponsor who would pay for a new boat, ideally a 50ft (15.2m) trimaran. Having failed to do so, he decided to take *Victress* – and was very much encouraged to do so by Eve, even though it would effectively make her homeless. He did manage to secure some sponsorship, however, from the record company Music for Pleasure. He planned to leave in September as soon as the Navy would let him.

Having failed to come to an agreement with regard to *Gipsy Moth IV*, Crowhurst decided to have a boat built specially for his voyage. At the end of June, however, *The Sunday Times* described him as somewhat mysterious, as he would reveal nothing about his new boat because he feared that his competitors might copy some of its revolutionary ideas.

In the same issue, Sir Francis Chichester justified the newspaper's role in the race by writing that, although it couldn't stop anyone who was determined to take part, it could offer advice to the competitors and try to monitor their positions so there would be a watching eye on them. By now, Moitessier was on his way from Toulon to Plymouth.

On 4 July, Alec Rose sailed into Portsmouth – to a 'tumultuous welcome' according to *Yachting World* – in his 36ft (11.0m) yawl *Lively Lady* having completed a solo circumnavigation with two stops: in Melbourne, as planned, and in Bluff Harbour, New Zealand, to repair a damaged mast. At a press conference soon afterwards, he was asked if he thought that a non-stop voyage was pushing things too far. He said that he didn't and that he 'felt on my arrival in Australia that I could have gone on without stopping'.

During the course of July, the port of Plymouth became quite crowded with Golden Globe competitors. Tetley and *Victress* were already there, of course, but they were soon joined by King's *Galway Blazer II*, Moitessier's *Joshua* and Fougeron's *Captain Browne*. The two Frenchmen were already friends but a sense of camaraderie soon built up between all four sailors, in a way that still endures amongst ocean-going single-handers to this day. Moitessier's preparations included removing anything he thought he wouldn't need in order to save weight – including the windlass, four anchors, a dinghy, a great many books and even the engine. While he was in Plymouth his wife Francoise drove nine times from the South of France and back, delivering stores and equipment and taking away unwanted gear.

Fougeron – strictly speaking not single-handed as he had his cat Roulis on board with him – and Moitessier both set sail from Plymouth on 22 August. King was ready to go that day as well, but as it was foggy he decided to wait. The following day was a Friday – unlucky in many sailors' minds as a day on which to start a voyage – and so he waited until Saturday 24 August before setting sail. By then, however, the favourable winds that the two Frenchmen had initially enjoyed had turned to the south-west, the direction in which he was heading. Moitessier was clearly happy to be under way.

> I feel passing through my whole being that breath of the high seas that once felt is never forgotten. What peace here in the open sea! And it seems ages ago that I stopped resenting the staff of *The Sunday Times*. In fact my rancour dissipated at Plymouth during our first meeting with the chaps who work on the paper.

Tetley's preparations continued, enormously helped by Eve. Although their task was considerably easier than that of the Moitessier's from a geographical point of view, converting *Victress* from a home into an ocean racing boat can't have been straightforward. *Victress* eventually sailed on 16 September with brass band music playing loudly from the deckhouse speaker and Tetley in tears.

Having argued that *Gipsy Moth IV* would be the best boat in which to race around the world, Crowhurst went from one extreme to the other and decided he would do it in a trimaran, despite the fact that he had never sailed one. There was also, of course, the issue of how to pay for it. Crowhurst's firm Electronic Utilisation produced the Navicator radio direction finder – one of several types on the market at the time – which he hoped would, at some point, make his fortune. The reality, however, was that the company was surviving precariously, and its main investor, Stanley Best, had told Crowhurst he wanted to pull out and that he wanted his money back. Undeterred and with extraordinary impudence, Crowhurst had written to Best on 20 May, and asked him to invest in his new boat. Best had made his money as a caravan dealer and perhaps it was Crowhurst's suggestion that the trimaran would soon become 'the caravan of the sea' that, against all the odds, secured Best's backing.

Crowhurst's new boat would be based on the same design as Tetley's *Victress*. The hulls would be essentially the same but several other features of the boat would be modified in an attempt to make her more suitable for the extremes of the Southern Ocean. She would have an almost flush deck with just a low doghouse instead of the more vulnerable superstructure that Tetley had, and Crowhurst also hoped this would give him a small speed advantage; she would have two extra cross arms (or beams as they would now be known) with corresponding extra bulkheads and with an upgraded method of joining them; and the deck would be twice as thick as standard. Not least because time was short, he commissioned two companies to build the boat: Cox Marine of Brightlingsea to produce the hulls and cross arms, and L.J. Eastwood of Brundall to assemble them and fit her out. Cox Marine completed their work, on time, on 28 July, at which point the hulls and cross arms were delivered to Brundall. Eastwoods were due to complete the boat by the end of August – a ridiculously unrealistic expectation, even without the countless modifications and additions demanded by Crowhurst. Inevitably the launch date was postponed through September and relations between client and boatyard became strained. This came to a head on 21 September over the issue of glassing the decks: Cox Marine had glassed the outside of the hulls and the specification called for the decks to be treated in the same way, but Eastwoods now revealed they had run out of time and had just painted them instead. Crowhurst was furious and that evening his wife Clare tried to persuade him to forget about sailing round the world and to refuse to take delivery of the boat. 'I suppose you're right,' he replied, 'but the whole thing has become so important for me. I've got to go through with it even if I have to build the boat myself on the way round.'

Just before she was launched, *The Sunday Times* reported that Crowhurst's boat would be three quarters of the weight of *Victress* and yet eight times as strong. Crowhurst was said to be designing a computerised system which, he hoped, would minimise the chances of his boat capsizing, but also allow him to right her in the event that she did. As she started to heel over, an alarm would sound and the sheets would be automatically eased. If the angle increased any further a CO_2 cylinder would inflate a buoyancy bag at the masthead, which would prevent her going upside down when the mast hit the water. He could then pump water into the upper float which would lower the whole boat until the main hull was in the water and the mast horizontal. The motion of the waves would then bring the boat upright again, and he would then pump the water out. Although it is thought that he took out a patent on this, it was one of the many systems he failed to put into commission before he started the Golden Globe race.

Although she was still very far from being finished, on 23 September the new boat was launched at Brundall and christened *Teignmouth Electron*. Crowhurst had recently met Rodney Hallworth – proprietor of the Devon News Agency and a Teignmouth resident – and signed him up as his publicity agent. Hallworth had then persuaded Crowhurst to start and finish his voyage from Teignmouth and to name his boat after the town, in return for which he would run a fundraising campaign in the area.

So it was that, on 2 October, *Teignmouth Electron* made her way under outboard engine down the River Yare to Great Yarmouth and then set sail for the south Devon coast. Crowhurst and his two crew expected this voyage to take around three days but it took thirteen, albeit two of which were spent storm-bound in Newhaven. There was generally a fresh wind dead against them all the way down the Channel, and Crowhurst found that *Teignmouth Electron*'s windward performance was dreadful. When they arrived in Teignmouth on 15 October with barely a fortnight before the Golden Globe starting window closed, there was still a massive amount to do.

By this time it was apparent that neither Wallerand – who was unable to prepare his boat in time – nor Howell would be taking part. Having finished the OSTAR in fifth place after more than thirty-one days at sea, Howell quickly sailed back, as planned, with the *Sunday Times* reporter Murray Sayle, who wrote that *Golden Cockerel's* self-steering gear was somewhat erratic, as a result of which Howell reluctantly withdrew from the Golden Globe race.

However, on 6 October, the newspaper revealed a new surprise entry: Alex Carozzo who was generally known as 'Italy's Chichester'. He had previously sailed a 33ft (10.0m) boat, which he had built in the cargo hold of a merchant ship on which he was serving, single-handed from Japan to San Francisco, even though he was dismasted along the way. But, for the Golden Globe race, he had commissioned the Medina Yacht Co. in Cowes, Isle of Wight, to build him a 66ft 6in (20.3m) ketch called *Gancia Americano*, more than 13ft (4.0m) longer than *Gipsy Moth IV* and a giant of a boat for a single-hander. He, too, had left things late, and the yard needed fifteen men working round the clock to ensure she could be launched on 8 October, just seven weeks after work began. Crowhurst met Carozzo just after *Gancia Americano's* launch when he was on his way from Great Yarmouth to Teignmouth and spent most of a day with him. He was particularly impressed by the Italian and his new boat, and thought he would be the one to beat.

The Sunday Times headline on 27 October announced that Crowhurst was ready to go. The newspaper reported that, despite his late departure, he hadn't given up the idea that he might be the first boat home as well as achieving the fastest time, and that, with a top speed of 15 knots he would still be in with a chance, particularly with favourable winds. In fact, some time before, Crowhurst himself had drawn up a table in which he listed each competitor's highest probable average speed, probable departure date, and resultant number of days at sea and arrival date. He thought his own average speed would be 9 knots, giving him a voyage time of 130 days and with it the £5,000 prize for the fastest time. Howell (who was still expected to take part at the time Crowhurst produced his table) and Tetley would be second equal with passage times of 146 days. Furthermore, based on a starting date of 1 October, Crowhurst would finish on 7 February, before anyone else and therefore win the Golden Globe trophy as well. It would be close, however, as three other competitors – Howell, Tetley and King – would finish within a week of him. It was absurdly optimistic in every way, mostly in terms of his own performance but with regard to everyone else's as well. He thought that Knox-Johnston, for instance, would finish on 3 March after 260 days at sea.

On the night of 30 October, Crowhurst and his wife Clare – who would be looking after their four small children by herself while he was away – stayed in a Teignmouth hotel. They had a late night as a farewell dinner had been arranged for him and, as they were lying in bed, he expressed concern that the boat wasn't ready and wondered how worried she might be when he left. 'If you give up now will you be unhappy for the rest of your life?' she asked. His only reply came from tears, and they lasted all night.

The next afternoon, barely seven hours before the Golden Globe deadline, Crowhurst set sail. *The Sunday Times* headline of four days earlier would prove to be woefully inaccurate in so many ways: he was a very long way from being ready.

Carozzo set sail the same day, or at least in terms of complying with the rules he did. He, too, was far from ready, and so he merely cast off and then picked up a mooring buoy off Cowes where he would continue his preparations.

Nine men had now officially started the Golden Globe race. Two, however, had already retired, and another two would do so within a couple of days.

Background to Ellen MacArthur's Voyage

It was just as Ellen MacArthur's new trimaran was about to be launched, in January 2004, that she and her team heard that Francis Joyon was about to set off on a solo circumnavigation in an attempt to beat the 93-day 3-hour 57-minute record held at that time by 2000/01 Vendée Globe winner Michel Desjoyeaux. Joyon's 90ft (27.4m) trimaran *IDEC* was already 17 years old and she had previously attempted five circumnavigations – and had been variously named *Charal*, *Lyonnaise des Eaux* and *Sport-Elec* – with Oliver de Kersausen, her skipper and owner, and a full crew in attempts to win the Jules Verne trophy. In the last of these, the attempt had been successful, when she finished after just over seventy-one days. Joyon approached the project on a limited budget: it is said that he chartered the boat relatively cheaply from de Kersausen, he didn't have new sails, he didn't employ a shore-based weather router and he even painted the name *IDEC* on the side of the boat himself, with a roller and when the boat was afloat. At that time just one person had successfully sailed a multihull solo and non-stop around the world and returned to port – Henk de Velde in a 70ft (21.3m) catamaran in 118 days in 1996–97 – and most people thought that it would be difficult to beat the existing monohull record without putting skipper and boat in great danger. However Joyon didn't just beat the record, he annihilated it, finishing in a time of 72 days 22 hours 54 minutes having sailed 27,150 miles at average of 15.5 knots.

'Can this record be beaten? … has he eclipsed his rivals for years to come?' ran the headline in *Yachting World* in April 2004. 'I hope I am going to give my successor some work to do,' Joyon himself said just before he finished. 'It was a fine challenge and I've set the standard quite high so that even with good funding it won't be easy to beat.' Soon after the finish, however, he said that another sailor could 'go out tomorrow' and beat his new record. In response to those who suggested that he had benefitted from more than his share of good luck with the weather, he said: 'My voyage wasn't without its share of misery and worry, but that's the daily fate of humanity'. After Joyon finished, his friend Rodney Pattison, the British three-time Olympic medallist in the Flying Dutchman class, presented him with one of his gold medals in recognition of his achievement.

MacArthur and her team heard about Joyon's success soon after her new trimaran – now named *B&Q* – had arrived in Auckland, from where further sea trials would be conducted.

When Joyon himself was later asked about MacArthur's chances, he replied: 'She is a very great sailor and I know she can beat this record. She has a wonderful boat … and I know she is very competitive.'

MacArthur was full of praise for Joyon's achievement. 'What Francis has done is extraordinary,' she said, 'he has set a stunning pace.' But it caused a re-evaluation of her chances of success and the general view within her team now was that, to beat this new record, she might have to have three or four attempts at it. She also took a very positive attitude to the situation, which was particularly noticeable in an interview with *Yachting World* just before she set off on her own attempt.

'I genuinely believe that, from a competition point of view, it's better,' she said. 'Before it was Mich (Desjoyeaux's) and it was, like, you're going to break a monohull record so what's the big deal? There was a record there but I was only a day off it in *Kingfisher*.'

Nigel Irens, the co-designer of *B&Q*, thought that to have beaten the monohull record would have been 'a doddle', and that Joyon setting his record had the advantage of creating a much higher profile for the attempt and that there was a lot more publicity to be gained.

Communications – 1968 and 2004

During the thirty-six years between Knox-Johnston's and MacArthur's voyages, unimaginable technological advances were made in a multitude of areas, a great many of which significantly affected the world of sailing. One of these was the ability to communicate. 'One of the greatest challenges facing the earliest solo circumnavigators was solitude and silence,' wrote Andrew Baker in *The Daily Telegraph* just as MacArthur's voyage was coming to an end, 'and one of the greatest advantages technology has bestowed on MacArthur is the ability to converse, in real time, with her shore crew.'

During her voyage MacArthur was in touch with the outside world every day, by both sat phone and email. She spoke to members of her shore team – mainly Mark Turner – daily. In an interview with *Yachting World*'s Elaine Bunting just before she set sail, she said:

Mark is 'that person' … we've been through so much together in the last eight years. He's someone on the end of the phone, someone you know is with you, going through every day with you. He's aware of what's going on, he looks at weather reports, he knows what's happening and he's aware of what mental state I'm in.

This regular communication allowed MacArthur's shore team to provide constant support, in the technical sense, for *B&Q* and also for the benefit of her personal morale and well-being. Information was regularly transmitted back to base with regard to the state of the boat (rigging loads, for instance, and much more) and MacArthur herself was fitted with various sensors to monitor and transmit her sleep patterns, blood pressure and heart rate. Much of the latter information was sent to a small medical team, including a doctor specialising in sleep deprivation.

MacArthur also regularly spoke to her family, including both her parents on Christmas Day. But she could 'hear the concerns in Mum's voice' and she was always aware that her family constantly worried about her. They always knew what problems she was experiencing – whether it was bad weather, breakages or lack of sleep – but they were helpless, All they could do was wait for further news and this constant communication often made things more difficult for everyone.

But it wasn't just her parents who knew when things were difficult for her. With twelve small cameras positioned around the boat, there were times when the whole world was able to watch. As Baker noted in his *Daily Telegraph* piece:

> When MacArthur has suffered, she has suffered in front of a massive audience, and the audience have responded with emails in their tens of thousands. There can be no other instance in sport of the protagonist being so close to the public for so long. It is ironic that when MacArthur was about as isolated as a human being can be, alone on a boat in the stormy Southern Ocean, her every move was watched by millions via the internet.

The emails of support came from all around the world and from all walks of life. She referred to some of these in an email which she sent to her shore team on day 39. 'I sat there reading people's encouragement,' she wrote, 'and quite honestly cried ... cried just to see the support of so many people from so many places. It's humbling – I feel like they must be for someone else doing something incredible.' By the sixtieth day of her voyage she had received 34,000 such emails and amongst those that arrived subsequently were two from very contrasting correspondents. The first was from Admiral Sir Alan West, the First Sea Lord, on day 64:

> We in the Royal Navy are enthralled by your progress in this ultimate challenge. In this special year for the Royal Navy as we commemorate the 200th Anniversary of the death of Admiral Nelson, and as a nation celebrate our rich maritime heritage, I am especially proud that we continue to have such outstandingly courageous and determined seafarers such as you.

And four days later 5-year-old Hope Reynolds wrote:

> I know that you are close towards the end of the race. Hope you win. Love Hope. PS Daddy tells me it's bed time now – I'll have some sleep for you because he tells me you are very tired now.

The day after MacArthur completed her voyage, BT was one of several companies who, quite understandably, placed advertisements in the national press to capitalise on her achievement.

> We made sure she was never on her own. BT was proud to provide Ellen and her management team with the vital communication solutions they needed ... High speed Broadband from BT enabled Ellen's communication team to send over a million email, video and photo updates almost instantly to people across the world.

At a press conference in Falmouth the same day, MacArthur said that 'the messages from school children, from soldiers serving in Iraq and people in America and Japan and everyone else have been incredible and very motivating.'

●—◆—●

But things were very different, of course, for Knox-Johnston and the other Golden Globe competitors thirty-six years earlier. Some of them didn't even carry transmitting radios and initially Knox-Johnston thought he wouldn't either. In view of their high cost, he would have settled for a small transistor radio that would have allowed him to receive news of the outside world and also time signals, which would be essential for accurate astronavigation. However, when the *Sunday Mirror* agreed to sponsor him, they insisted that he should be able to transmit regular reports, so he installed a new Marconi Kestrel II high-frequency set which, he later found, had a range of 3,000 miles.

The two Frenchmen were among those that didn't have transmitting radios. Moitessier later wrote that the 'big cumbersome contraptions were not welcome' while *The Sunday Times* reported that, because he didn't want the extra bulk and distraction of wireless equipment, the paper had provided him with flares, a loudhailer and a catapult. These would allow him to attract the attention of passing ships, and then catapult messages to them which would be relayed via Lloyds. The newspaper also provided him (and Fougeron and Tetley) with special waterproof plastic bags that had been developed with the help of a company called Envopak Ltd who were said to be specialists in that kind of product. These allowed the competitors to pass exposed films, logbooks and diaries to any other vessels with which they came in close contact. The bags had messages silk-screened on to them in four languages asking that they should be sent back to the newspaper. Moitessier later wrote that the *Sunday Times* photographer he met in Plymouth:

> was sorry that I preferred my old, quiet friend the slingshot to two or three hundred pounds of noisy radio equipment ... but he helped me to find good rubber bands, supplying me with aluminium film cans to contain messages I would shoot on to passing ships. A good slingshot is worth all the transmitters in the world!

A simple system of communication between vessels at sea which was particularly useful in those days, before the development of more sophisticated and readily available electronic devices, involved three International code flags: M, I and K which, when flown together, meant 'please report my position to Lloyds of London'. *The Sunday Times* provided all competitors with six sets of these flags – enough, it was hoped, to last all the way around the world with a set displayed at all times.

Moitessier's first attempt to pass a package to another vessel almost ended in disaster. In mid-October he was off South Africa and he planned to sail in to Walker Bay, about 50 miles south-east of Cape Town, where he hoped to find other small yachts out sailing. However, he decided that, as it was blowing very hard, that was unlikely, so he turned his attention to a small Greek freighter called *Orient Transporter* that looked as if it would pass close by. He successfully catapulted a message onto the ship's foredeck asking that it should come closer so that he could pass over a larger package. 'One of the officers twirls a forefinger at his temple, as if to say I must be a little nuts to be shooting at them,' he later wrote. The freighter then came to within about 10 yards, which allowed Moitessier to throw his package across, but then it came too close and actually made contact with *Joshua*, breaking two of her shrouds and bending her steel bowsprit by more than 20 degrees. 'Ship runs down Moitessier,' read the *Sunday Times* headline when the incident came to light more than two months later. Happily, though, as Moitessier himself wrote a couple of days after it happened, he was 'able to repair my boat, as solid and beautiful as she was when I left Plymouth.'

Tasmania would provide Moitessier's next opportunity to pass on news of his progress and, he hoped, hear something about his competitors. As he approached the island just before Christmas, he constructed two model boats to carry messages. One was a 4ft (1.2m) long catamaran that he built from 'two bits of purau, a very light wood that had been kicking around the forepeak since Tahiti,' he later wrote. 'She is square rigged with a black sail visible from a distance and a white jib with "message" written on it.' The other was a 2ft (0.6m) long ketch 'cut from a piece of Styrofoam sandwiched between two sheets of plywood. Her hull lines are not bad at all; she has a masthead jib and a lead keel so she cannot capsize.' He attached a plastic bottle containing a letter and photographed extracts from his logbook to the deck of each boat 'wishing the finder a happy New Year and asking him to forward the mail. Life would be pretty sad if one didn't believe in Santa Claus from time to time.' He cast these two model boats adrift when he was about 200 miles west-south-west of Tasmania but initially 'they head south where there's no one. But I know they will steer north, towards land, when the right time comes.' Amazingly, both these model boats were found over a year later – one on the shores of Tasmania and the other in New Zealand – and the messages were perfectly readable.

Realistically, however, Moitessier knew that he could by no means rely on these messages getting through at any time, so he headed towards Tasmania. Initially he thought that he would sail into a cove where he would leave a plastic container – also supplied by *The Sunday Times* for this very purpose – with 'message' written clearly on it, and anchor it in the hope that it would be found later. Instead, he happened to come across a small fishing boat with three people in it, and was able to pass over a roll of film to them.

But Moitessier was clearly a big fan of the model boat method of communication:

Ideally, Loick and I would have left Plymouth with shipments of little plastic boats. We could have launched a whole flotilla when rounding Good Hope, Australia, and New Zealand, with films of the log. Loosed every half day on port tack with lashed tiller, many would have got through, without our taking the risk of flirting with land.

Or Greek freighters, he might have added! He did, however, become very frustrated with the lack of news about his competitors, especially the three that he had befriended in Plymouth, and he seems to have been particularly unhappy with the BBC World Service in this respect. 'Perhaps the BBC is against the idea of such a voyage being run as a race,' he wrote. 'So how about it? Four friends leave about the same time to sail non-stop around the world and nobody lets them know about each other.'

Donald Crowhurst, the electronics engineer, initially intended to take a radio transmitter that he had built himself but this was vetoed by the GPO. So, during the chaotic fortnight of his final preparations in Teignmouth, Marconi engineers worked through several nights to install a new Marconi Kestrel set. The generator that was needed to provide the power to, amongst other things, run the radio was installed under the cockpit. Crowhurst had insisted that it should be fitted there to keep its weight down low for the benefit of the boat's safe sailing performance, but its only access was through a hatch in the cockpit sole. Crowhurst could reasonably expect large volumes of sea water to be regularly dumped in the cockpit during his voyage, and for that reason the hatch needed to be completely watertight – however, it would be found to be woefully lacking in that respect.

Crowhurst also had on board a number of forms printed on Teignmouth Urban District Council paper which read:

From Donald Crowhurst, sailing alone non-stop around the world. The bottle containing this message was placed in the sea at .... hours on .... 196 .... My position being .... and my log reading .... miles.

It finished with an address to which any finder should send it. Crowhurst's plan, as a publicity stunt, was that he would, at regular and appropriate intervals, fill in the blanks on a form, seal it in a bottle and throw it overboard. It is not certain whether he ever did so.

Before Knox-Johnston set off, he agreed with Bruce Maxwell at the *Sunday Mirror* that they would make regular contact by radio on Thursdays. This worked fairly well as *Suhaili* made her way down the Atlantic, initially through the GPO station at Baldock, Hertfordshire and then, from 27 July, through Cape Town. On 11 August, Maxwell revealed that these radio conversations had taken on another dimension as he and Knox-Johnston had been playing chess, each of them making a move on a weekly basis, although he thought that the solo sailor had recently made a couple of suspect moves. Later that month the Soviet Union invaded Czechoslovakia, and Maxwell was despatched to Prague to cover that story. The chess game continued, however, and Knox-Johnston's next move – king's knight to castle four – was sent from *Suhaili* to Prague via Cape Town and London. Maxwell felt obliged to send a message to any suspicious Soviet agents in Prague that it really was just a game of chess and not a secret code.

At the beginning of September, *Suhaili* suffered a knockdown soon after she entered the Southern Ocean. Amongst the resulting consequences was water damage to the radio. The problem was an intermittent one at first but it soon became worse, and by the end of the month, when he was about halfway between Cape Town and Perth, he was unable to make contact with the radio stations in either city. 'Solo Sailor Is Silent' read the headline in the *Sunday Mirror* on 6 October, while Knox-Johnston's father was quoted as saying that he and his family were not in the least bit worried about him.

When he was about 500 miles from Australia, he began to pick up Australian radio stations – and found that he got to know details of the Albany wool market particularly well – but was still unable to transmit. Realising that his only hope of making any sort of contact with anyone was to encounter another vessel – just as Moitessier and others had planned to do from the start – he soon took a more northerly course in the hope that he might see one. He was suitably rewarded on 25 October. When he first saw the coaster *Kooringa* she was about 3 miles away, and he managed to attract attention by firing his rifle. *Kooringa* altered course and came within about a cable of *Suhaili*, giving Knox-Johnston the opportunity to signal 'all well' by Morse code on his fog horn. He was also flying his MIK code flags and he got the impression that the *Kooringa's* crew realised who he was and he hoped the news would soon reach home. It did, and was reported in the *Sunday Mirror* two days later.

In early November, he sailed through the Bass Straits, between Tasmania and mainland Australia, and it was there that he managed to encounter the Melbourne pilot vessel *Wyuna* and pass over a package with rolls of film and diaries giving further news of his voyage so far. The following day several aircraft flew over – one of them while he was sunbathing naked – indicating to him that he was becoming big news.

The package passed to *Wyuna* included a letter to the *Sunday Mirror* suggesting a rendezvous off Bluff on the southern tip of New Zealand and that was where *Suhaili* then headed.

As he approached Bluff, Knox-Johnston heard on New Zealand radio that there was bad weather coming, but he hoped to reach shelter before it arrived. He didn't, however, and he soon realised that he would have to beat towards Bluff in a force ten and against a foul tide. He decided that a change of plan was called for and headed around the bottom of New Zealand's South Island and up towards Otago. The only chart he had was of the whole of New Zealand's South Island with no detail whatsoever, and when he was just outside the harbour entrance he found himself aground and on a falling tide. *Suhaili* was stuck on a sandy bottom but Knox-Johnston stripped off and jumped over the side with an anchor, which he dug in to prevent the boat drifting towards nearby rocks when she re-floated. Back on board, he was close enough to the shore to easily converse with people there and one of them agreed to go off and find Bruce Maxwell, the *Sunday Mirror* reporter, who was probably looking for *Suhaili* in Bluff.

While he waited, Knox-Johnston found himself 'enjoying a cigarette and appreciating the quietness' as he later wrote. He also struck up a conversation with some people in a runabout called *Sea Witch*. 'I had forgotten how pleasant company was, and I could have sat listening to them for a week.' He took advantage of *Suhaili's* relative stillness to climb the mast to sort out a problem with the main halyard sheave. While he was up there, he continued to converse with *Sea Witch's* crew who brought him up to date with world news, including the Mexico Olympics about which he was particularly keen to hear. They thought that Britain had won sixteen gold medals: a woeful exaggeration as the country's final total was just five.

By the time Maxwell arrived late that night, *Suhaili* was floating again – having been aground for five hours – but was still at anchor. The two of them started chatting – Knox-Johnston on board *Suhaili* and Maxwell on shore – but the first message from the reporter was a great disappointment. Knox-Johnston was desperate for news from home and, although Maxwell was able to tell him that his family was well, he was unable to give him any mail. He explained that the rules had been changed, or at least tightened, in that no material assistance of any sort was allowed. To be on the safe side, he had assumed that this included mail and so he hadn't brought any. Knox-Johnston later wrote that he 'felt very disappointed at this and pretty bloody angry too, at what I considered then, and still do now, a rather childish and unnecessary restriction.' After the two of them had chatted for an hour or so, Maxwell went off to phone his office in London, with the intention of coming back to resume the conversation. However, while he was gone, changing weather conditions gave Knox-Johnston some concern, so he set sail again.

It was 21 November and nothing more would be heard of Knox-Johnston – nor would he hear virtually anything about the progress of his competitors – until the beginning of April. When he was about 900 miles east of New Zealand, he had an indistinct radio conversation with someone in Chatham, but it was so unclear that he thought it very unlikely that the person on the other end knew who he was. Just over halfway to Cape Horn, he managed to pick up an American commercial station from which he learned that the Apollo 8 spacecraft was just about to return to Earth after orbiting the moon ten times, the first manned mission to do so. 'The contrasts between their magnificent effort and my own trip were appalling,' he later wrote. 'I was doing absolutely nothing to advance scientific knowledge; I would not know how to.'

On 9 January, eight days before he rounded Cape Horn, he heard on Voice of America that the Chilean navy had been asked to look out for a 'damaged ketch' battling towards that famous landmark. Soon after he rounded the Horn he made repeated, but failed, attempts to make contact with Port Stanley in the Falklands and Punta Arenas in the Magellan Straits. But on one occasion he did at least hear 'English voices loud and clear and I almost hit the deckhead with excitement'. It was a British Antarctic radio station's 'chatter hour' which Knox-Johnston was able to enjoy listening to for ten consecutive evenings.

Having failed to make any radio contact, Knox-Johnston was keen to sail towards Port Stanley to let people know he was alright. However, he calculated that the subsequent headwinds would have added a couple of days to his voyage, and so he decided not to. Elsewhere in the South Atlantic, he spotted a ship which was too far away to make contact, but on 10 March, just north of the equator, he had better luck – or so he thought. He saw a ship coming towards him at night time and tried to make contact, first by signalling with his Aldis lamp, then with a handheld flare and more signalling, and then with a distress rocket. After a further signalling attempt, the ship gave a token answer and then steamed away, ignoring the fact that Knox-Johnston had indicated he was in distress. He was furious.

Over the following days, he saw a number of other ships, two of which came within half a mile, but none answered his signals. 'This was a shattering revelation to me,' he later wrote. 'I was trained as a merchant seaman to understand that keeping a lookout was the primary duty of the Officer of the Watch when at sea.' On 2 April, when he was about 600 miles south-west of the Azores, he sighted a Norwegian cargo ship. He hoisted the MIK flags and as the ship got nearer he fired three rifles shots and then two more. The two vessels passed within about 150m of each other. It wasn't until they were abreast of each other that the ship's Officer of the Watch appeared to notice *Suhaili*, but still didn't bother answering Knox-Johnston's signals.

Three days later he managed to make contact with the British tanker *Mobil Acme*, on her way from the Thames to Texas. They exchanged signals with their Aldis lamps and within two and a half hours his family knew he was safe and so too, very quickly, did the nation. 'Robin Is Safe,' read the headline on the front page of the *Sunday Mirror* on 6 April, and 'Tanker Spots "Lost" Sailor' in *The Sunday Times*. Knox-Johnston's father was quoted as saying that it was 'tremendous news' but that he never thought he wouldn't turn up as he was such a good sailor. While his mother used the same adjective, it seemed that she might have been less confident: she described the news as 'a tremendous relief'.

Knox-Johnston, however, still had no news of his competitors. For that he would have to wait another week, until 12 April when he made contact with another ship, the Le Havre-based *Mungo* with which he was able to have a conversation on a short-range frequency. The following day he somehow managed to get through to the GPO station at Baldock and they patched him through to his family home where his brother Mike answered the phone. 'I'm told he nearly went through the roof,' Knox-Johnston later wrote. He also spoke to his mother and his foster sister Diana, although his father was out at the time. Mike was able to give more news of his competitors but 'the best news was that all the family was well. It is often forgotten that the worrying is not only confined to those left at home.' Nine days later, Knox-Johnston arrived in Falmouth.

Both Chichester and Knox-Johnston had mixed feelings about radio contact. During the early part of his voyage, when his radio was still working, Knox-Johnston wrote in his log: 'I had a most unsatisfactory day. I always do when I have been in radio contact. I get excited by getting through and then the feeling of anti-climax follows, and I feel depressed.' And on 27 April, in an interview with the two circumnavigators which was published by *The Sunday Times*, Chichester said that he didn't particularly like having to talk on the radio. He said that he only did it to satisfy his sponsors and that each time he made contact with someone he found it upsetting afterwards.

It might be easy for some to think that the communication issue made MacArthur's life much easier than Knox-Johnston's, but consider Sue Mott's words in *The Daily Telegraph*, published the day after *B&Q* returned to Falmouth:

Obviously she was helped by high-tech gadgetry. So is Michael Schumacher in his Ferrari cockpit but few call him a lesser sportsman for all that. MacArthur lives in an age when communication is instantaneous. It may be more romantic to contemplate the circumnavigations of Sir Francis Chichester or Sir Robin Knox-Johnston when man battled with the mind-altering effects of genuine solitude and the sea. But MacArthur's is a 21st century feat with all the wizardry that goes with the time. It does not diminish her courage. Nor should it lessen our admiration for someone who embarked on this journey as a yachtswoman and returns as a symbol of human aspiration.

Choice of Boats

Before Knox-Johnston decided to build a boat in India, he and a colleague, Peter Jordan, considered buying a dhow with a view to sailing it back to England. Common sense prevailed, however, when they realised how difficult it would be to then sell it, and so they began to contemplate a boat which would be a better investment, with a view to using it for underwater photography and skin-diving on their way home, and then selling it for a profit.

They agreed that a ketch-rigged family cruising boat capable of ocean passages would suit them best and, after carrying out some research by reading sailing magazines, they ordered a set of plans from a company in Poole, England. The company's claims that they offered 'full plans and a free advisory service' proved to be somewhat false as, not only were the plans that arrived for the wrong boat – 'a somewhat old fashioned but very seaworthy boat,' Knox-Johnston later wrote – but the rigging plan was by no means complete. But time was short – the following year's north-east monsoon season presented a very real deadline – and so they decided to build to the plans they had received. At that time Knox-Johnston had no idea who had originally produced the plans, and it wasn't until after his circumnavigation that he discovered that *Suhaili* was based on a 1924 design by the American William Atkin.

Work began in November 1963. The new boat was built entirely in Indian teak and with very substantial scantlings: 6in (150mm) square stringers and 1¼in (32mm) thick planking, for instance. She was also produced entirely with hand tools, using the same traditional methods that previous generations of Indian shipwrights had used to construct Royal Naval ships, including HMS *Ganges* in 1821. 'We would watch, fascinated,' Knox-Johnston later wrote, 'as the adze, handled almost casually by the Indian craftsmen, produced as fine a scarf as any modern plane.'

The 2¼-ton iron keel was cast in two sections, the spars were made of Kashmiri pine and a 38HP BMC Captain diesel engine was installed. This engine – and many other pieces of equipment, such as the winches, toilet, the wire and rope for the rigging, and the sails – had to be sourced from the UK but the potential problem of shipping them out to India was solved when Jordan, returning from a spell on leave in England, was given permission by the British India company to bring them with him while working his passage.

Knox-Johnston had hoped to set sail by September 1964 but the construction didn't go as quickly as expected, and it wasn't until 19 December that the new boat was launched. In accordance with local tradition, a coconut was cracked over her bow, and she was named *Suhaili*, which is the name given by Arab seamen in the Persian Gulf to the south-east wind.

Soon after *Suhaili* was launched, Jordan had a change of plans, as did Mike Ledingham, another colleague who had contributed to the build costs, and so Knox-Johnston bought their shares after borrowing the money from his family to allow him to do so. The total cost of the boat was £3,250, which was about two years' salary for Knox-Johnston at that time. On the first leg of *Suhaili*'s voyage back from India, she leaked very badly and so, at the first port of call in Muscat, Knox-Johnston had three steel floors fabricated and he fitted them in the forward part of the boat where none had been called for in the design. They were installed while *Suhaili* was alongside a rusty barge at low water as there was no slipway available.

By the end of the voyage back to England, Knox-Johnston had good reasons to be pleased with the performance of his new vessel:

Suhaili had proved herself a seaworthy boat, able when close-hauled to sail herself for long spells without attention because of her remarkable 'balance'. There was too much weight aloft in the masts which caused her to heel over alarmingly at times but she was tough, safe, and at an average speed of 112 miles a day, faster than we expected.

When, in March 1967, Knox-Johnston started to contemplate a solo non-stop circumnavigation, he ruled out doing it in *Suhaili*. 'She was too small and, even though I knew her now and she was part of me, I could never hope to race Tabarly in her.' He decided that he would need a new boat and that would require him to sell *Suhaili* or find a sponsor, although the reality is that it would probably have required him to do both. He would need a boat that was 'robust, seaworthy, long on the waterline … and ridiculously cheap to construct. This of course is what every prospective boat owner is after: the impossible for the ridiculous.'

The following month he put *Suhaili* on the market and went to visit the naval architect Colin Mudie to explain what he wanted. Within a week Mudie produced some preliminary plans for a 53ft (16.1m) steel yacht, with a schooner rig consisting of two identical Dragon masts which would be relatively economical and would allow a sharing of spare parts. Knox-Johnston then approached a number of boatyards for quotations but he got little or no satisfaction from all but one – some gave him a shockingly high price while others refused to quote at all, but eventually he found a yard in Woolwich that quoted him £2,800 for the hull. He considered this to be very reasonable and that it would allow him to complete the boat for a total of £5,000, which he thought would be 'fantastic'. He still needed to get hold of that money, however (as well as another £2,000 to pay off his loan on *Suhaili*) and so he began to look for a sponsor, writing more than fifty letters to potential companies who might be interested in helping him. However, during the course of the summer, not only was there still no buyer for *Suhaili*, but the potential sponsors' rejection letters were coming steadily in.

During this time, he gradually came to realise what he must do. 'Everything led to the obvious answer,' he wrote. 'Go in *Suhaili*.' One significant advantage in doing so was that he wouldn't need to carry out extensive sea trials in her in the way that he would with a new boat. On the other hand she needed a fair amount of work – new sails, a new mizzen mast (to reduce weight aloft and one which he hoped he would be able to 'manhandle about the boat in case the mainmast broke'), new rigging, a self-steering system, caulking and painting – which, he thought, would cost in the region of £1,500. He didn't have the money to do that either. But his luck eventually changed in the middle of January 1968 when he secured a book deal with a publishing company. The book would be written by Knox-Johnston at the end of his voyage and the advance allowed the refit work to go ahead.

Suhaili has a hull length of 32ft 6in (9.9m), but her length-over-spars is 44ft (13.4m). Her ketch rig carries an upwind working sail area of 666sq.ft (62sq.m). Although Knox-Johnston would have preferred a bigger boat, after his circumnavigation he wrote that, apart from her length, she was 'an ideal boat for the voyage'. He particularly liked her double-ended hull form which meant that she was rarely pooped. 'Although it would have been nice to have had a faster boat, in the Southern Ocean it is safety and not out-and-out speed that counts.' Others made comments which, on the face of it, may have seemed uncomplimentary, but there was an element of respect behind them. A harbour official in Falmouth, for instance, described *Suhaili* at the start of her voyage as 'a real old icebreaking boat. If she hit England I'd be concerned for England'; and a year later Jack Knights wrote in *Yachts & Yachting*, in an article entitled 'All Hail *Suhaili*', that she was 'the most old-fashioned, unsleek (untarty, Knox-Johnston would probably say) four-year-old yacht one can possibly imagine' and that she was 'about as comfortless as a horse drawn bus and even slower.'

Tetley's and Crowhurst's choice of trimarans for the Golden Globe was, to put it mildly, controversial. Any yacht being raced competitively needs, at all times, to have as much sail up as the prevailing wind allows, and it only takes a sudden gust of extra wind for it to be immediately overpowered. An alert crew will normally be able to react quickly enough to minimise the consequences, by easing sheets or altering course, but a single-handed sailor may well be asleep or tending to other needs. Any small yacht can be capsized by strong winds or by big seas, but there is a fundamental difference between a monohull, which is extremely likely to quickly right itself thanks to its ballast keel, and a multihull, which is almost bound to remain upside down.

Chichester himself – who had, at that time, more experience of sailing a small yacht in the Southern Ocean than anyone else – expressed concerns when delivering a lecture to the Royal Institution in January 1969.

> Without continuous expert helmsmanship, I think a multihull is at serious risk in the vast seas and strong winds liable to occur in the Southern Ocean, of being bowled along on the surface like a piece of thistledown and of ending upside down.

In the summer of 1967 when Bill Howell was racing his catamaran *Golden Cockerel* across the English Channel, she was caught by a sudden gust with too much sail up and he capsized. Howell was lucky enough to be rescued and he later described the event as 'the best thing that ever happened to me' as he had survived and he was able to learn from the experience. That winter, according to *The Sunday Times*, he fitted an emergency release system for the sheets so the wind could quickly be spilled.

With regard to the anti-capsize/self-righting system that Crowhurst designed for *Teignmouth Electron*, although most of its component parts were fitted – including the buoyancy bag at the masthead – they were never connected to each other, and so it was never commissioned.

However, while Chichester was expressing his fears to the Royal Institution, Tetley was about halfway around the world. In fact, a couple of weeks earlier he had made radio contact, through Perth Radio, with Dr Francis Smith, the president of the Western Australian Trimaraners Association. Concerns had also been raised regarding the safety of trimarans in that part of the world and with good reason: five boats had been lost in the previous year with the loss of fifteen lives. Tetley's voyage – which was already considerably longer than any multihull had previously been sailed solo non-stop – was making a major contribution in supporting the cause of multihull fans.

During the second week of January, *Victress* went through some particularly bad weather – with winds up to Force 11 and 12 – south of Australia, but came through it with very little damage. In a radio call soon afterwards, Tetley said:

> I am quite convinced there has never been a more exacting test of the trimaran. This has absolutely proved the multi-hull concept. She is perfectly

seaworthy and been riding these waves like a rock. I could have gone faster, but I would sooner be sure of being alive.

On 2 March 1969, when Tetley was about three weeks away from rounding Cape Horn, *The Sunday Times*, in a piece entitled 'Trimaran's Final Test'. speculated on this impending historic event. 'The trimaran has still not satisfied the purists of its ability to master the roughest seas,' the report read, 'and Tetley rounding the Horn in his 40ft *Victress* could well be the ultimate step towards making the multihull "respectable".'

After Moitessier rounded Cape Horn, he wrote – by no means for the first time – of his concerns that he had heard no news of his 'comrades', the other three competitors who he had befriended in Plymouth. He was particularly worried about 'Nigel, so vulnerable in his trimaran. These things can capsize and you can go whistle trying to right them.' He also wrote that he and Fougeron had tried to persuade Tetley to take:

> a good sharp saw with plenty of set to keep it from binding in damp wood. In case he capsized he could cut off one of the hulls and continue on his merry way to land on a sponson-turned-canoe. A trimaran sponson makes a nice little boat, and would probably sail very well … Nigel would have none of our large economy-size saw; he thought we were kidding.

As it happens, Tetley successfully sailed *Victress* around the world, in the sense that his homeward path crossed his outward one, although he failed to sail her back to port. Derek Kelsall, a friend of Tetley's who would become a successful designer and builder of multihulls, said that he could 'think of nothing that was right about that boat for that race' and that *Victress*'s circumnavigation was never recognised for what it was – 'a truly remarkable effort in a most unsuitable craft.'

Between 1969 and 2003, when Joyon set off on his circumnavigation, just four people successfully sailed a multihull around the world single-handed:

Alain Colas in 1974 in the trimaran *Manureva* in 201 days, with one stop for repairs
Philippe Monnet in 1987 in the trimaran *Kriter Brut de Brut* in 129 days, with one stop for repairs

Olivier de Kersauson in 1989 in the trimaran *Un Autre Regard* in 125 days,
   with two stops for repairs
Henk de Velde in 1997 in the catamaran *C1000* in 118 days, non-stop
   Lisbon to Brest.

Despite the extremely limited history of circumnavigating solo multihulls,
their design and development had come a very long way since Tetley's time,
and so for MacArthur the decision regarding the number of hulls became
reasonably straightforward. 'A monohull with the required performance
would be too big to handle by one person,' she explained in an interview
with *Yachting World*'s Matthew Sheehan in April 2004, 'and it's not on to
expect an autopilot to steer a cat when it's flying a hull.'

Multihull specialist Jeremy Evans, writing in *Yachts & Yachting* in February
2005, agreed with MacArthur's view that a trimaran is better for a single-
hander:

A cat is in no danger while it stays flat, but once it flies the windward
hull things can go rapidly wrong and lead to a capsize. By comparison, a
trimaran can heel over and spill some wind, helping maintain equilibrium.
The trimaran will also perform better than a cat when under or over
powered – very important for a solo sailor who cannot perform rapid
sail changes.

It was obvious, then, that she needed a trimaran.
   With that in mind, she deliberately started racing on other people's
multihulls, including *Foncia*, on which she described the learning process as
'vertical'. At that time, *B&Q* had already been designed, so it was really just
a question of confirming that the project should go ahead, but after *Foncia*'s
capsize off Portugal in May 2003, she expressed concern with regard to the
speed at which things can change on a multihull, from everything being OK
'to finding your world quite literally upside-down'. She began to consider
how her new trimaran – now under construction in Australia – could be
improved with regard to the possibility of a capsize. Just as Bill Howell had
thirty-six years earlier, she recognised her own capsizing experience as an
opportunity to learn valuable lessons.

By the time MacArthur and her team learnt about Joyon's attempt, and resulting success, on the round-the-world record, it was much too late to make anything but the most minor changes to B&Q, but Neil Graham, the team's technical director, claims it wouldn't have made any difference anyway:

> Clearly Francis Joyon has now raised the bar with an impressive performance, but we were already under way with drawings and plans before we even knew he was making an attempt on this record and even though his boat is 90ft long to our 75ft, we still wouldn't change anything even if we were starting again from scratch.

B&Q was designed by Nigel Irens and Benoit Caberet who, as *Yachting World* reported in April 2005, had been 'a major force in ORMA 60 trimarans for many years, and some of the key elements of B&Q's design come from the lessons learnt in that fleet.' However, the designers were unrestrained by any sort of measurement rule, such as that which governs the ORMA 60s, and so they were able to design specifically for the task ahead, particularly for a safe but fast passage through the Southern Ocean.

In an interview with *Yachting World* in June 2003, Irens also described further compelling reasons why a trimaran would be better than a catamaran:

> The three-hulled configuration, by definition, should have an advantage in the light stuff coming through the lower latitudes. Cats have a lot of wetted surface in those conditions and tend to get very sticky. Part of the problem is they have a fair amount of waterplane area – the cross section through the waterline. That means they respond to all the changes of levels of waves around them and the rig is always being shaken about and it never really seems to settle down and really get going. In that respect, a tri is a bit more like a monohull in that it leans over a bit and doesn't have too much wetted surface or too much waterplane area and seems to make better progress.

At 75ft (22.9m) – the longest that it was felt that MacArthur could realistically handle – B&Q is 15ft (4.6m) longer than ORMA 60s, and all this additional length is in the very buoyant bows which were intended to minimise the chances of pitchpoling. She had a reasonably pronounced rocker to help manoeuvrability while at the same time the longitudinal separation between the centreboard (which is forward of the mast) and the rudders would help directional stability. The beams linking the three hulls were particularly arched to maximise wave clearance.

Although the component parts of B&Q were produced in six different countries – for instance: the spars in New Zealand, the foils in the UK and the sails in the USA – the hulls and beams were built by Boatspeed in Sydney, Australia. In the engineering of the hull, valuable lessons were learnt from earlier multihulls, particularly those which had taken part in the storm-ravaged 2002 Route du Rhum, many of which suffered significant structural failure. They had been built with honeycomb carbon panels, which were so stiff that they were unable to withstand the shock loads caused by wave impact. B&Q was, as Yachts & Yachting put it, 'almost retro by comparison, with foams and balsa in the hulls and rigid honeycomb only used in the deck.'

After a build time of eight months – and, reportedly, 30,000 man-hours – B&Q was officially launched on 8 January 2004. On the same day, by virtue of a satellite link, MacArthur officially opened the London International Boat Show – the first to be held at the ExCel Exhibition Centre after almost half a century at Earls Court – from Sydney. Matthew Sheehan of Yachting World joined the boat for one of the sea trials which took place in Auckland soon afterwards, and his first thought was how difficult it was just to get under way. 'It took seven people several minutes to raise the mainsail to the hounds by bouncing the halyard,' he wrote, 'after which there was a back-breaking grind on the pedestals for two that took a further couple of minutes.' It was later reported that it took MacArthur around thirty-five minutes to hoist the 137kg mainsail by herself.

Sheehan also described tacking the boat, which involved:

[Around] six separate operations all of which require grinding. Furl the genoa, tack the boat, unfurl the genoa and sheet in. Then pull the mainsheet up the traveller and sheet the main in before going around the cycle once more to fine-tune the trim.

And all this was soon to be done by just one person. Crucially, however, that person was very reassured by these trials. In particular, she was pleased by the directional stability – especially in comparison to ORMA 60 trimarans – which accompanied the boat's obvious speed and power.

Sheehan described the power as 'awe inspiring', and wrote how:

> [With] each 20 knot gust the boat speed leapt to 23 knots. As it did so the noise below decks sounded like the rush of air that precedes the arrival of a train in an underground station. To break records this will be the pace Ellen needs to keep up for days on end. It's a sobering thought.

MacArthur's early favourable impressions stuck with her. After she delivered the boat from the Falklands to New York, she wrote that although 'Mobi' was physically hard work to sail, she was also rewarding in a number of ways. The autopilot steered her well in a variety of conditions, she coped well with big seas and she was very different to sailing *Kingfisher II*.

Not everyone was happy about MacArthur's choice of boat, however. 'I've never been very happy about multihulls,' her mother Avril was heard to say when *B&Q* arrived safely back in Falmouth at the end of her circumnavigation.

●◆●

As *B&Q* and *Suhaili* are such vastly different boats, it is almost meaningless to compare their vital statistics. Nonetheless, consider this: while their displacements are fairly similar – 8.3 tonnes and 9.7 tonnes – *B&Q*'s working sail area is around four times that of *Suhaili*'s.

Falmouth

Up until the mid-seventeenth century, the main town in the area that is now Falmouth was Penryn, at the top of the Penryn River. Falmouth, by comparison, was very small, but that began to change in 1688 when it was appointed as a Royal Mail packet station. Falmouth was chosen in spite of its 270-mile distance along very poor roads from London because it was (and still is) the nearest sheltered, deep-water harbour of any size to the Western Approaches. This allowed the packet ships to transport their valuable mail and messages from England to various places around the world – initially to the Iberian Peninsula and the Mediterranean, but later across the Atlantic to Halifax, the West Indies and South America – and to do so with the minimum of interference from the French, with whom England was at war for much of this time. In the mid-nineteenth century it was, however, inevitable that Falmouth's days were numbered in terms of the packet service, as the development of faster and more reliable steam ships allowed much quicker and easier access to London, especially in unfavourable weather. The last packet ship sailed from Falmouth on 6 December 1850.

Robin Knox-Johnston's initial plan was to start his voyage from London, but he changed his mind and decided to start from Falmouth for two reasons. The first was because a passage through the Thames Estuary past Dover and down the English Channel would involve sailing through a particularly busy area of shipping which would require him to keep a really good lookout at all times. 'I would have to keep awake for at least two days just to avoid shipping,' he later wrote, 'which would leave me very tired right at the beginning and, I hoped, at the end of the voyage.' The two days he anticipated might easily be extended if he experienced westerly winds which was quite likely, whereas from Falmouth he would be able to clear the main shipping lanes considerably more quickly. 'The second reason,' he wrote, 'was curiosity – I had never been to Falmouth.'

He later came to the conclusion that 'Falmouth as a port of departure was a better choice than I could have imagined.' He greatly enjoyed the hospitality there, particularly that of Bob and Di Drennan who ran the Marine Hotel where he stayed:

[They] took us completely under their wing. We would wander in and out at all times of the day or night, dirty and tired, and always they or Neil Andrews the chef, wold produce meals or something hot to drink as if it were the most natural thing in the world.

Before he set sail, he booked a room for his return, with the intention of giving his landlords a better idea of the date when he was off Australia.

'Falmouth, the scene of so many sea sagas,' reported the *Falmouth Packet* a few days after *Suhaili* set sail, 'Was the starting point for yet another great maritime adventure at the weekend'.

• ◆ •

The factors when considering a starting port for MacArthur were quite different. Her official starting point for her record attempt was a line between two countries, and to gain easy access to that line there were a number of ports, on both sides of the Channel, she could have used. Final preparations to *B&Q* – including removal of her engine and the loading of stores – were actually made in Lorient, a fair bit closer to the southern end of the start line

– almost certainly the favoured end – but she chose Falmouth because, she said, 'it was easy logistically'.

She, too, came to realise that she had made a good choice, later writing that she was 'overwhelmed' by the 'outstanding send-off'.

It was by no means a foregone conclusion that she would also return to Falmouth after she crossed the finish line, however. But when she and her team discussed the matter during the course of her voyage, it seems it was an easy decision. Under the headline 'Falmouth – The Only Place To Be' in *The West Briton* newspaper three days after she finished, she was quoted as saying: 'The reception when we first arrived was fantastic. We were so well looked after. During the voyage we were discussing it and we decided we should go back to where it all started.'

Departures

Robin Knox-Johnston wanted to spend as little time as he could in Falmouth before setting off around the world, as he wanted to give himself as much of a lead as possible over the faster boats which he expected to start after him. As it happens, he was there for five days which he later described as 'chaotic'. A radio engineer from Marconi came on board to give the radio a final check, several small metal fittings were fabricated by a local company, *Suhaili* was dried out against the harbour wall at Mylor to allow Knox-Johnston and a friend to check the underwater caulking and apply a coat of antifouling, and a host of other last-minute jobs were carried out. *Yachting Monthly* later reported that Knox-Johnston's 'quiet and unassuming manner did more to ease the usual last minute search for chandlery etc. than a more brash approach would have done.' The night before he set sail, the Marine Hotel threw a party for him which lasted until the small hours of the morning, allowing Knox-Johnston just three hours' sleep before he awoke with a hangover.

On Friday 14 June, Knox-Johnston brought *Suhaili* alongside to fill her water tanks, and the Port Chaplain came to visit him. At this point, he realised he had left his Bible at home so the chaplain offered to go and buy him one.

The Daily Mirror's Bruce Maxwell had spent much of the time in Falmouth helping with *Suhaili*'s last-minute preparations. He later reported that Knox-Johnston had always been jocular, even off-hand, about his forthcoming voyage but that, on the morning of departure, his manner changed. 'The smile was still there but his face was drawn, tense and he had suddenly become much quieter,' Maxwell wrote.

For Knox-Johnston, the hardest part about leaving was saying goodbye to his parents, who had come to Falmouth to see him off. They did so, along with his younger brother Mike, in a motor boat which escorted *Suhaili* out of Falmouth Harbour, and from which Knox-Johnston senior called 'Good luck son, I'll see you back here next year'. The solo sailor responded with a smile and said that, as there was very little wind at the time, it would take two years at the speed he was going. His mother remained tight-lipped and was heard to say that she thought he was mad to do it but that she would have to get used to the idea.

During the conversation that Knox-Johnston had with Francis Chichester soon after the end of his voyage, he said:

> The day I left I jolly nearly didn't go. I just looked at my parents and I could see they were upset and I was pretty scared too. I felt should I be doing this? Is it fair to them? But I knew I wanted to do it and felt I had to do it.

'I think a man is built in a certain way,' replied Chichester, 'and that if a man has in his blood the urge to do this sort of thing he must do it, or he is not living his proper life.' Soon after that conversation, Knox-Johnston wrote that, when his parents and friends turned back towards Falmouth and left him to get on with his solo voyage:

> it was a rather shattering moment as the first feelings of true loneliness came to me. I began to wonder what I should be like in a week's time if I felt like this now, and I wished I knew how I would react to being alone for long periods.

Almost twenty years later, writing in *Classic Boat,* he added:

> [Naturally] … had doubts when I left Falmouth in June 1968: was *Suhaili* large enough to survive the enormous seas in the Southern Ocean? Was I capable of staying the course? Could any boat stay in one piece for almost a year without maintenance? No one could give me answers to those questions, the only way to find out was by trying.

But now he was under way and simply had to get on with it, and when he was just a few miles out of Falmouth, he got out his charts and began to plan his route for the first time. 'It may seem to be one hell of a time to be doing this,' he later wrote, 'but there was no need for such detail before.'

•◆•

Whereas Knox-Johnston was keen to leave Falmouth as quickly as possible, MacArthur had different priorities. She needed to start in the weather conditions that she and her shore-based weather router considered would be as favourable as possible for the early stages of her voyage, and so she would wait as long as was necessary. As it happened, MacArthur and *B&Q* were on standby in Falmouth for over a fortnight.

During that time, MacArthur visited the National Maritime Museum Cornwall – which had only opened the previous year and which was adjacent to *B&Q*'s mooring – where she was given a tour by museum director Jonathan Griffin. As part of the tour she was shown a display of some of her own memorabilia from her 2000/01 Vendée Globe voyage: her gloves, the novels she read and miniature bottles of champagne she opened at significant stages of the course. She also visited Falmouth School and welcomed some of its pupils aboard *B&Q*. According to the *Falmouth Packet* newspaper, she 'captured the hearts of Falmouthians during her stay in the port.'

She herself regarded her time in Falmouth as being 'a bit like being stuck in limbo'. She wrote of the difficulties of mentally preparing for a race with an unknown start time until, that is, the time is suddenly set with perhaps only a couple of days' notice.

She passed the time and kept her mind focused by going running in the local countryside.

When the time came to leave, she, too, found it particularly hard to say goodbye to her parents. In fact, she did so on the phone, from a room in the maritime museum. The three of them decided that it would be easier if they didn't say their goodbyes in person on the pontoon as it would be too difficult for all of them, not least the difficulty of knowing what to say. But in her final words she told them that she loved them and she tried to be reassuring about the voyage ahead.

'Ellen walked quietly to her trimaran,' it was reported in the *Falmouth Packet*, 'accompanied by officials before waving goodbye to hundreds of well-wishers and being towed out into the Carrick Roads. Many more people cheered from Pendennis Point.'

B&Q cast off from her berth at around 4 p.m. on 27 November 2004 but, unlike Knox-Johnston, MacArthur's solo voyage didn't officially begin as she left Falmouth. That would happen early the following morning when she crossed the southern end of the Lizard–Ushant start line, and so for the next few hours she was accompanied by a crew, and during the evening she took the opportunity to grab some sleep. When she awoke she initially 'felt normal', until she remembered where she was and what she was about to undertake. She later wrote that, for the first time at the beginning of a solo voyage, she 'felt sick with nerves and frightened', not least because she would be truly alone and not sharing a conventional start line with a number of other solo sailors who were going through the same experience. Turner came into the cabin to tell her that it was time for him and the rest of the crew to get off the boat into a waiting RIB, and the two of them just hugged as 'words were not necessary'. She sobbed relentlessly as she watched the RIB disappear into the distance. 'This for me was without doubt the loneliest moment of the record,' she later wrote.

• ◆ •

At dawn on 28 November, MacArthur was in sight of Créac'h lighthouse at Ushant and, after checking with her weather routers that the forecast was still favourable, she crossed the line at 27 knots in a strong northerly wind at just after 8.10 a.m., with helicopters filming her from overheard. By mid afternoon *B&Q* was on the same latitude as Les Sables d'Olonne from where twenty other solo sailors had started the Vendée Globe just three weeks earlier.

'MacArthur gets flying start to her record bid,' read the headline the next day in *The Daily Telegraph*, which also reported a message from Francis Joyon from his home in Brittany. 'I wish Ellen good luck for this big adventure,' he said. 'May the conditions be favourable to her on this course (which is) so wonderful but also so difficult.'

The Golden Globe

On 17 June 1968, three days after Knox-Johnston set sail from Falmouth, John Ridgway was off Madeira where he met up with Bill Gardner, a reporter from *The People*, who came out to meet him in a small chartered boat. They conversed for a while and then they exchanged various items: exposed films and diaries from Ridgway and newspapers, letters and Madeiran foodstuffs from Gardner. As Ridgway departed they agreed on another rendezvous at Bluff on the southern tip of New Zealand's South Island. Soon afterwards, Ridgway read the copy of *The Sunday Times* that was included in Gardner's delivery, and he realised that he was now technically disqualified from the race as he had broken the rules by receiving the supplies (including the newspaper itself) from Gardner. He was furious and thought this was a ridiculously petty ruling, but he sailed on anyway.

Blyth, meanwhile, was a few hundred miles behind him and had been having trouble with his radio transmitter. He still hadn't got to grips with the rudiments of celestial navigation.

Knox-Johnston averaged just over 70 miles a day during his first week, but on the seventh day he at last managed 100 miles. On 24 June, he had his first swim of the voyage. This was something he would do numerous times throughout his circumnavigation – for exercise and recreation – when the water was warm enough and when *Suhaili* was going sufficiently slowly. He would stream a warp from the stern, jump over the side at the bow and then try to race the boat until she overtook him and he was alongside the warp, which he would then grab to haul himself on board.

On 30 June, *The Sunday Times* published position reports of the three boats that were now at sea. John Ridgway was said to be increasing his lead over his two rivals and, according to his sponsoring newspaper *The People*, he had passed close to Madeira on June 16, fifteen days after his start from the Arran Isles; Chay Blyth, who had started a week after Ridgway, had cabled his wife in Cowplain, Hampshire, on the 26th to say he was then off Madeira; Robin Knox-Johnston had reported to his sponsor the *Sunday Mirror* that he hoped to pass the island the next day, which would be two days slower than Ridgway and one faster than Blyth. Ridgway was said to be averaging about 86 miles a day and his competitors 10 to 15 miles fewer. By comparison, two years earlier Sir Francis Chichester had passed Madeira eight days after leaving Plymouth.

On 1 July, Blyth experienced his first gale. His self-steering gear simply couldn't handle it and nor, for that matter, could he when he tried to steer himself. This was the first real indication as to the unsuitability of Blyth's boat for the task ahead. He dropped his sails and began to read the manual of sailing he had on board to see what he should do. 'It was like being in hell with instructions,' he later wrote.

The following weekend, *The Sunday Times* reported that, two days earlier, *Suhaili*'s position was about halfway between Madeira and the Cape Verde Islands. The newspaper thought that Knox-Johnston must have substantially improved *Suhaili*'s performance and that he was now likely to catch up with Ridgway and Blyth unless they had managed to find a way of getting more out of their own boats.

On 10 July, Knox-Johnston sailed between Santo Antao and Sao Vicente in the Cape Verde Islands, where he found the wind significantly increased. At the time he was doing about 7 knots with the spinnaker, staysail and mizzen up and although he thought that he should probably reduce sail he 'decided the thrill was too good to miss'.

Almost a week later, *English Rose IV* was about 600 miles south of the Equator, sailing close hauled on the port tack, when Ridgway noticed that the port side-deck was flexing in way of the chainplates. Fearing he could lose his mast, he dropped the sails and tried to affect a repair by installing a more substantial plywood backing pad. However, this made little difference. He was convinced that this possibly imminent failure had been caused by the collision with the fishing boat when he left Inishmore six weeks earlier, despite the fact that it had been not much more than a glancing blow and had occurred on the opposite side of his boat. The reality was that this family cruiser was woefully inadequate for such extended ocean sailing. He now realised he would have to retire from the race but, to some extent, not with any great regret as he had been miserable for almost all of the six weeks he had been at sea. Nonetheless he wrote, with a heavy heart, in his logbook: 'I don't think I have ever given up in my life before. Now I feel debased and worthless.' It was an entirely sensible decision, however, as – notwithstanding the problem with the port chainplates – *English Rose IV* would never have survived the Southern Ocean as he was now realistic enough to admit. He wrote in his book *Round the World with Ridgway* (which was mostly about a subsequent successful circumnavigation) that:

It would be easy to say I would have won the race but for the damage (I had started a week before my nearest competitor and over two months before the last) but I don't think I would have made it anyway.

He now pointed *English Rose* towards the Brazilian coast.

Ridgway arrived safely in Recife on 21 July, and on the same day *The Sunday Times* reported that Knox-Johnston's progress had been slow. That week he had covered half his previous week's distance due, it seemed, to the Doldrums extending further north than would be expected at that time of year. There had been no news of Ridgway or Blyth for several weeks.

Suhaili crossed the Equator on 27 July and the following day the Sunday newspapers had news of Ridgway's retirement. *The People* reported that he had been battered by 'mountainous seas and gale force winds' (something of an exaggeration), and *The Sunday Times* said that he felt terrible, as he had failed himself as well as all those who had helped him with his preparations. 'Just tell them I'm sorry,' he said. Still nothing had been heard of Blyth, however, although this was not necessarily a matter of concern as the radio he was carrying had a very short range.

A week later *The Sunday Times* reflected on Ridgway's retirement and speculated that it might signify a similar, or worse, outcome for Blyth – who began his voyage in something of a rush, with very little single-handed experience and in a boat which was not dissimilar to Ridgway's – and for Knox-Johnston

On 11 August, Knox-Johnston's sponsor the *Sunday Mirror* published a piece showing great support for their man. Bruce Maxwell wrote that he was 'streaking ahead in the race to sail non-stop round the world' and that this 'lanky 29-year-old Kent yachtsman in his 32ft ketch *Suhaili* has an excellent chance of being the first man to achieve this feat.' This was despite the fact that Blyth's whereabouts were still unknown and that the other boats which were about to start were known to be significantly faster.

But a few days later Blyth surfaced. One of the problems he had experienced was that salt water had contaminated his supply of petrol, which meant that he couldn't run his generator, charge his batteries, or use his radio. So he decided to call in to Tristan da Cunha – a volcanic island on about the same latitude as the Cape of Good Hope and just over 1,500 miles to the west – to see if he could obtain some fresh petrol there. As luck would have it, he found a ship, the *Gillian Gaggins*, anchored there and delivering fuel from South Africa – which it did just three times a year – and he moored alongside. He genuinely thought that if he received petrol from the ship he would not be breaking the Golden Globe rules as long as he didn't go ashore but, of course, he was wrong. In fact, he received much more than just petrol, including an offer of hospitality from the captain – a fellow Scot, as it happens – which eventually included a glass or two of whisky, a shower, a night on board the ship and a good breakfast. It was here that he first learned of his former rowing partner's retirement from the race.

After breakfast, it suddenly became apparent that the warp with which *Dytiscus III* had been moored to the *Gillian Gaggins*'s stern overnight had parted and there was then a frantic rescue to prevent her going ashore. As soon as Blyth was back on board his own boat, he hoisted the sails and went on his way.

On 22 August, when he was approaching the South Africa coast, Blyth made contact with a passing liner on her way to Cape Town. He managed to hand over his logbook to her with the request that it should be sent on to his wife. On that same day, Moitessier and Fougeron set sail from Plymouth, and *Suhaili* was about 250 miles north of Tristan da Cunha. Knox-Johnston learned of the two Frenchmen's departure in a radio call to Cape Town almost immediately.

Blyth had been becoming increasingly aware of the unsuitability of *Dytiscus III* for such a voyage. Not only were there signs of breakages and damage on board for him to see all too clearly for himself, he also knew that Ridgway's boat, which had ultimately let him down, was of a similar type. For this reason, he now began to push the boat harder than he knew was sensible, and for a good reason. He wanted to test her thoroughly before he entered the Southern Ocean – where conditions would be considerably tougher – while he was still within range of South Africa, where he might be able to seek shelter if something significant went wrong.

Moitessier was sighted by a ship just south of Lisbon on 29 August, and four days later, *Suhaili* crossed the latitude of 40 degrees South and therefore officially entered the Southern Ocean. Within two days Knox-Johnston found out just what a treacherous part of the world this can be when *Suhaili* was knocked flat. He was about 800 miles south-west of Cape Town and, although he had been concerned about the weather, he had managed to drift off to sleep – it was night time by now – with his self-steering gear seemingly in control. He was awoken, however, with *Suhaili* pinned on her side and a great many items of stores and equipment on top of him as he lay in his bunk to leeward. She soon came up again, however, and he rushed on deck to see what damage there was, fully expecting to see that the rig had gone. Luckily it hadn't, but there was other damage – to the self-steering gear, for instance – and an almighty mess down below where there was water above the sole boards and stores and equipment strewn everywhere.

Blyth had damaged his self-steering gear too, and he would need spare parts for it if he was to continue. He managed to get a radio message through to home, thanks to a passing ship, asking for these parts to be sent to East London on the south-east coast of South Africa, and that was where he now headed. He later wrote of his reasons for wanting to continue with his voyage:

What it amounted to was that the thing I was still curious about was me. The boat, simply because I had taken it where it had never been intended to go, had failed ... But I still did not know if I myself could stand up to

the circumnavigation – and if I could find out, then I wanted to do so …
Provided I could go on without being foolhardy, I wanted to see the thing
through. It was my voyage of self-discovery, and what I wanted to discover
was me.

On 8 September, the *Sunday Mirror* reported that Knox-Johnston had
managed to repair *Suhaili*'s self-steering, and two days later when he was
due south of Cape Town, he wrote in his log that he had 'covered a fantastic
314 miles in two days'.

Blyth arrived in East London, South Africa, on 13 September and remained
there for four days. *Dytiscus III* lay alongside the dock and Blyth was joined
for much of the time by Chick Gough, a former paratrooper friend who now
lived in South Africa. The two of them drank whisky and beer which Gough
provided. Eventually the spare parts arrived and Blyth set sail. Crucially – as
far as Blyth was concerned – he never left the boat during that time, but that
didn't change the fact that he had blatantly broken the Golden Globe rules
once again.

Nor was he going to get away with it. While he was still in East London, on
15 September, *The Sunday Times* reported that Blyth would be disqualified,
not only for taking on board the spare parts in East London but also for
receiving outside assistance from the *Gillian Gaggins* in Tristan da Cunha.

The judges needn't have bothered with this official ruling, however,
because, just two days after leaving East London, Blyth was caught out in
a strong gale – with winds estimated at 60 knots and seas which he later
described as 'colossal' – and he came to the final conclusion that *Dytiscus III*
was definitely not the right boat in which to continue. He turned back to
Port Elizabeth where, a short time later, his wife joined him to help him sail
back up the Atlantic to home.

There was also news of other competitors in the 15 September issue of
The Sunday Times.

Bill King, who had left Plymouth on 24 August two days after the two
Frenchmen, had become the first competitor to overtake one of his rivals.
Four days earlier, he reported that he was passing the Cape Verdes while,
on the same day, *Captain Browne* was sighted 350 miles south-west of the
Canaries, about 500 miles behind *Galway Blazer*. Moitessier hadn't been
seen or heard of since 1 September when he was about 150 miles north of
the Canaries. There had been no word from Knox-Johnston for almost as

long but the newspaper considered that, with the retirement of Chay Blyth, he should be in the lead. The following day Tetley set sail from Plymouth, and three days later Knox-Johnston was able to make contact with the *Sunday Mirror* and report that he was about 1,200 miles east-south-east of Cape Town.

Meanwhile Fougeron had been having trouble with his cat Roulis. She had eaten her way through electrical cables, including the radio aerial wire, and had managed to open a packet of egg powder, which she then spread around the boat. Furthermore, she had fleas and Fougeron also suspected that she might be pregnant. So, on 20 September, when he encountered a fishing boat off the Cape Verdes, he handed over Roulis, along with a plastic bag containing exposed film and letters to be sent on to *The Sunday Times*. The following weekend, the newspaper published a photo of Roulis along with the story of the chaos she had been creating.

Fougeron explained in his notes to the newspaper that, to his great sorrow, he was going to have to send Roulis ashore. She was initially handed to the British Consul in the Cape Verdes, but he couldn't cope with her destructive nature either and arrangements were soon made to send her to a friend of Fougeron's in Belgium.

On 29 September, Moitessier arrived at the island of Trindade – about 800 miles east of Rio de Janeiro – where he hoped to encounter a vessel to which he could pass film and mail to be sent on to *The Sunday Times*. However, he didn't dare go too close as he didn't have any detailed charts of the island – in fact he had forgotten to take his copy of the Brazil Sailing Directions which would have included detailed information about Trindade ('not a smart move,' he later wrote) – but he hoped to attract the attention of some people ashore, if not another vessel. For an hour or so he sailed up and down the coast blasting his foghorn until, suddenly, more than twenty people emerged from a building. But they seemed to simply just stare at him, and so – after repeatedly dipping his MIK flags – he soon realised he was wasting his time and he began to sail off. At that point the islanders ran down to the beach and, it seemed, tried to gesture for him not to go, but as they didn't seem to have any sort of boat in which to get out to him, he continued on his way. 'Still waving, the arms get further and further away,' he later wrote. 'The shouts from shore begin to blend with the rumble of the sea as *Joshua* rushes towards the horizon. I feel as though I want to cry!'

Having sailed from Plymouth on 16 September, *Victress* reached a point about halfway between Madeira and the Canaries on 3 October. When reporting this three days later, *The Sunday Times* stated that Tetley was frustrated as he was sailing in very light winds. The following week the newspaper reported, as far as it could, on the positions of all five competitors now at sea. King had told the *Daily Express* the previous Wednesday that he was about 100 miles off Brazil and halfway between Recife and Rio de Janeiro; the next day Tetley made radio contact with *The Sunday Times* when he was 80 miles north of the Cape Verdes and had been sailing in excellent weather conditions; Moitessier had not been heard of for almost six weeks (the world knew nothing of his Trindade encounter at that stage) and Fougeron for nearly three; and Knox-Johnston was well on his way to Australia. The latter might well have been a rash assumption given that there had been no word from *Suhaili* for a fortnight when she had been barely a third of the way from South Africa to Australia.

Moitessier next came to light on 20 October when he rendezvoused with the Greek freighter *Orient Transporter* in Walker Bay, South Africa. He had hoped, in vain, that this would give him the opportunity to get some news of the three competitors with whom he had become friends in Plymouth: Fougeron, King and Tetley. 'Their names have not been mentioned once in the BBC overseas broadcasts,' he later wrote. 'Where are they?'

Moitessier's Walker Bay rendezvous allowed *The Sunday Times*, a week later, to publish predicted finishing dates for each of the five boats currently at sea, based on their last known positions. *Captain Browne*, however, hadn't been heard of since 20 September when she was 600 miles north of the equator, and *Victress* since 17 October when she was 400 miles north of the equator, but the other boats' positions had been reported in the previous three days: *Joshua* was still very close to the South African coast, *Galway Blazer* was about 1,700 miles west of Cape Town, and *Suhaili* was in the Australian Bight, about 300 miles east of the longitude of Cape Leeuwin. Based on this information, *The Sunday Times* estimated that *Joshua* would be first home, arriving on 24 April, followed by *Suhaili* (10 May), *Galway Blazer* and *Captain Browne* (both on 26 July) and then *Victress* (1 Aug).

Around this time, King heard on his radio about Moitessier's progress and immediately realised that he had little chance of winning either the Golden Globe trophy or the cash prize. 'Already I face the same sort of emotional situation that must have faced Scott when Amundsen reached the South Pole first,' he wrote in his logbook.

On 31 October, Donald Crowhurst's *Teignmouth Electron* set sail and Alex Carozzo's *Gancia Americano* picked up a mooring off Cowes. There were now seven Golden Globe competitors 'at sea', the most there would be at any one time, although those maximum numbers would not last very long.

On that same day, *Galway Blazer II* and *Captain Browne* were caught in a ferocious storm in the South Atlantic: the same storm, as it happens, as the two boats were only about 300 miles away from each other. In the early hours of the morning, *Captain Browne* was hove-to and Fougeron was trying to rest. Suddenly, his boat was hit by a massive wave which turned her on to her side and put her masts in the water. When she came up again, Fougeron rushed on deck, terrified of what damage he might find. Amazingly, however, he found that the rig was intact, albeit somewhat damaged. He was enormously relieved, but he immediately decided that he would retire from the race and head for Cape Town.

A few hours later, *Galway Blazer* was running downwind under bare poles but, when the wind suddenly changed direction and began to cause a particularly confused sea, King decided she might be better off lying ahull. That evening, just as he thought the worst was over and he had opened both deck hatches, she was rolled over on to her side. 'Hurled by the elemental forces of the breaking peak of a rogue sea mountain,' he later wrote, 'she was using her side as a surfer would his board.' He was confident, however, that soon enough the weight of her ballast keel would come into force and she would come back up again, until, that is, 'a vast new force started to act upon us' and there followed 'the mariner's most dreaded catastrophe: a complete rollover, upside down.' Momentarily he became convinced that she wouldn't come back up again, but very soon she did. His first priority was to pump out the substantial amount of water that was now inside the boat and, as soon as he did so, he went on deck to inspect the damage and was shocked by what he saw: the foremast had snapped off about 12ft (3.66m) above the deck, the main mast was very badly damaged, and the self-steering wind vane was also in a sorry state. He was extremely lucky though, because when the boat capsized he had been in the relative safety of the cabin, but moments before he had been on deck trying to resolve a minor issue with the self-steering and he gone down below briefly just to fetch a sail tie with which he would stow a sail more securely. For the second time in one day, a Golden Globe competitor made the decision to retire – not that he had any choice in the matter – and head for Cape Town. But first he had to erect a jury rig from what remained of his spars, and then he began the long slow journey to Cape Town, over 1,000 miles away. Along the way, he wrote a heartfelt message in the logbook, which was initially intended for his wife's eyes only:

> As the danger receded, I get broody. I realise the cold facts. My voyage has been stopped. My little boat lies broken, and I am alone with my bitter disappointment, creeping along at perhaps 50 miles a day. I knew such an adventure must be dicey, but I never gauged how shattering a blow this disaster could deal my spirit.

Meanwhile, Knox-Johnston had been having problems with his self-steering gear and on 3 November, when he was about 300 miles from Melbourne, 'it packed up for the third and last time'. He briefly contemplated retiring but soon ruled that out. But he needed to see how he could manage without his self-steering, otherwise he would have to steer himself for sixteen hours a day and then heave-to when he wanted to eat and sleep, something he was seriously thinking he might do. Having, at that time, sailed about 32,000 miles in *Suhaili* since she was built, he knew her sailing characteristics very well and was confident that she could sail herself ably when on the wind. The fact that she had a long keel (which gave her directional stability), and a ketch rig (which could provide a variety of sail options for balancing her in different conditions) was all positive, and he now began to experiment with various sail configurations so that she could do the same on other points of sailing. By the time he was halfway across the Tasman Sea, 'it was beginning to look as if it might be possible to continue the voyage ... *Suhaili* was balancing so well that the long stretch across the Southern Pacific no longer seemed quite so formidable.'

As it happened, *Suhaili* would sail the rest of the way around the world with no working self-steering gear. Although in certain conditions Knox-Johnston found that he had to do more steering himself than he would have liked, for the most part his continuing experiments with *Suhaili*'s balance paid dividends.

On the same day that *Suhaili*'s self-steering finally gave up the ghost, *The Sunday Times* reported King's capsize and subsequent damage, but not

Fougeron's. There was no recent news about him, and nor was there any of his compatriot, although the newspaper speculated that, at his current rate of progress, Moitessier could be off south-western Australia by 20 November.

At the end of the first week of November, *Suhaili* sailed through the Bass Strait between Tasmania and mainland Australia. He wrote later:

> [I] felt pretty happy as I sat steering through the rather choppy sea … Here
> I was, just about half-way round the world, the third and smallest boat to
> make the voyage. Civilisation was just over the horizon, and I began to be
> tempted by the thought of a sound sleep in a soft, unmoving bed, a large
> steak, and company … I kept thinking that no one had got farther than
> this, so why not pull in, there were plenty of reasons over and above the
> self-steering packing up. But I knew this wouldn't do, and I'd never forgive
> myself if I did not try to go on.

His encounter with the pilot vessel *Wyuna* allowed the Sunday newspapers to give their readers an update. 'Troubles all the way … but Robin sails on into history,' read the headline in the *Sunday Mirror*. The article said that he had become the first man to sail single-handed from England to Australia and then keep going, and that the diaries he had passed to the *Wyuna* 'tell us a mixture of great hope and utmost despair – in brief the agony of the long-distance sailor.'

The Sunday Times, meanwhile, reported that Knox-Johnston and Moitessier were 'locked in a duel of seamanship and stamina in the Golden Globe race … the dogged Briton has decided to hold his position over the Frenchman – with or without self-steering gear, with or without sleep.' The newspaper also published the estimated finishing dates for the competing boats but, as there had been no further news of Fougeron (word of his retirement had still not got out), Moitessier or Tetley since the previous predictions two weeks earlier, their dates remained unchanged. But they were now saying that *Suhaili* would finish two days later than previously, on 12 May, and declined to make any sort of predictions for Crowhurst or Carozzo, whose voyages were barely under way.

Carozzo had stayed on his mooring off Cowes carrying out further preparations for about a week before actually setting sail, but on 14 November – when he was about 150 miles west of the north-west tip of Spain – it became apparent that he had a serious problem. Unlike his competitors, however, it wasn't with his boat. In a radio call to *The Sunday Times* he revealed that he had been vomiting blood. The newspaper arranged for him to talk to a doctor who then diagnosed that Carozzo had an ulcer, a complaint from which he had, apparently, previously suffered. But Carozzo then reported that the bleeding had stopped and he was feeling better and would press on while keeping to a careful alcohol-free diet.

On the same day, *Teignmouth Electron* was a little further south of *Gancia Americano* off the coast of Portugal. Crowhurst had all sorts of problems with his woefully unprepared boat – a faulty radio, leaking deck hatches in the port hull as well as the cockpit sole, bilge pumping problems, poorly cut sails, poor stowage arrangements, unreliable self-steering, and so on – and his daily progress had been about half that which he had hoped for. 'I've never put to sea in such a completely unprepared state in my life,' he said into an on-board camera. He was giving serious thought as to whether he should continue – on 15 November he wrote almost endless reams in his logbook regarding the advantages and disadvantages of doing so. 'What a bloody awful decision,' he began, 'to chuck it in at this stage – what a bloody awful decision!' Amongst other things, he wrote of the unacceptable odds – 50 per cent, he calculated – of surviving in the Southern Ocean. He considered various options including turning back or pressing on and at least trying to make it as far as Cape Town or Australia. In the end he decided to keep heading south and to make the decision another time. The next day he sent a telegram to Hallworth in which he was deliberately vague about his position. 'Going on towards Madeira,' the message ended. As it happens, he was still several hundred miles from Madeira but Hallworth wasn't to know that, and he merely interpreted Crowhurst's words in a way that was appropriately positive for a PR man, and the resulting reports in the press were that Crowhurst was 'near Madeira'. This would be an ongoing theme – Crowhurst's vagueness or economy with the truth and Hallworth's over-optimistic interpretation – throughout *Teignmouth Electron*'s voyage.

That weekend, *The Sunday Times* reported that there had been no more news of Tetley since 17 October despite three attempts by Cape Town radio station to contact him. The article ended with a paragraph of speculation by Captain C Rich, the navigation instructor at Sir John Cass College, who calculated that Fougeron could have rounded the Cape of Good Hope five days ago and Moitessier might reach Cape Leeuwin, Australia, within a few days. The fact that Moitessier and Tetley hadn't been heard of for a month, and

Fougeron for two, didn't stop the newspaper printing a diagram indicating what each boat's average daily mileage might be so far: *Joshua* 129.5, *Victress* 92.1, *Suhaili* 89.3, *Captain Browne* 88.1, *Gancia Americano* 82.1 and *Teignmouth Electron* 78.0.

Moitessier continued to hunger for news of his Plymouth friends. When he was about halfway across the Indian Ocean, he wrote that:

> Since I left Plymouth I've been listening to as many English- and French-speaking radio stations as I can, hoping to get news of Nigel, Bill King and Loick. I haven't heard anything about them, but I have been listening to a lot of political talk from many different countries. What a laugh! Now I really understand why so many people just turn their backs and go away when political leaders open their mouths.

News of Tetley came through at last on 19 November when he managed to make contact with Cape Town radio after six weeks of radio silence. He was about 800 miles west-south-west of Cape Town. On the same day, news of *Suhaili* passing New Zealand reached Crowhurst just as he was sailing very slowly around in circles about 100 miles north-east of Madeira, wondering whether he should stop there. Eventually, however, he decided to carry on. Two days later he spoke to Stanley Best and told him that, because of the leaking hatch in the cockpit sole and resultant generator problems, he might not be able to make contact for a while.

On 21 November, *Suhaili* set sail again after Knox Johnston's rendezvous with Bruce Maxwell off Otago, and the next day *Galway Blazer II*, with her jury rig, arrived safely in Cape Town. The *Yachting Monthly* correspondent Argus later wrote that King had 'seemed the least unlikely ... to fail in the tremendous task of completing a single-handed, non-stop, unassisted circumnavigation,' and added that 'It is hard to believe that anyone is going to win this Golden Globe.'

That weekend, the *Sunday Mirror* reported on a new record broken by their man, as he had now sailed further without stopping than any other single-hander. Bruce Maxwell, fresh from his meeting with *Suhaili* off Otago, reported that Chichester had sailed 15,517 miles on the Sydney–Plymouth leg of his circumnavigation and that Knox-Johnston, who he assumed was now between New Zealand and Chatham Island, had sailed 15,700 miles.

'The week it all happened,' read *The Sunday Times* headline the same day and went on to describe the previous seven days as 'in some ways the most heart-breaking and certainly the most exciting … of the "Everest of the Sea" round-the-world yacht race.' The main news was that Carozzo had been forced out of the race by his own health issues. Whatever 'careful diet' he had adopted hadn't worked and his medical condition had taken a turn for the worse. He had radioed this news the previous day and had reported that he was practically becalmed about 40 miles south-west of Oporto. Portuguese emergency services had been put on alert but his exact position was a mystery, as a Portuguese Air Force DC6 had failed to find him. There was mention of two new records: Knox-Johnston's, as reported in the *Sunday Mirror*, and another by Tetley, who had now sailed several thousand miles more than any other solo multihull sailor.

Although there had been no word from Moitessier for over a month, the newspaper reported that by now he should have passed Cape Leeuwin and be somewhere in the Great Australian Bight, while there was still no word of his compatriot's retirement, and so it was assumed that he should have rounded the Cape of Good Hope.

The article then turned its attention to the possible outcome of the race which, it was thought, 'looks like developing into a gripping duel between the courageous Englishman, Robin Knox-Johnston, and the older and more experienced Frenchman, Moitessier.' It was thought that *Suhaili* would round Cape Horn in mid January and *Joshua* about three weeks later, and that the Frenchman would then continue to make gains and would finish on 24 April, just six days before Knox-Johnston. But the paper conceded that 'such a small difference is well inside the possible error of such calculations, and the Golden Globe race is clearly neck-and-neck.'

It wasn't long before the Portuguese air search located Carozzo. He was about 15 miles away from Oporto and, although he had been determined to make his way there without help, there was not a breath of wind, so he accepted a tow from a pilot boat. On 1 December, *The Sunday Times* published a photograph of him in a hospital bed awaiting an operation. He thought that his ulcer had been brought on by the enormous mental and physical strain of building and preparing his boat in such a short time. 'I was on edge and not in right frame of mind,' he explained, and when talking about his decision to retire after it became apparent that he wasn't well, he said: 'I am a bloody fool to try to sail around the world alone, but I am not a complete idiot.' He had heard that King was thinking of making another circumnavigation attempt and he said that he was also interested in doing so. 'I want to keep in touch with *The Sunday Times* to see if another race can be arranged next year.'

A few days later, at last, news came through of Fougeron's retirement. Although he had initially decided to head for Cape Town, head winds led to a change of mind and so he made his way towards the tiny South Atlantic island of St Helena, and it was there that he eventually arrived on 27 November. On the same day, Tetley wrote in his log that 'an almost overwhelming temptation to retire and head for Cape Town is growing inside me – the cold finger of reason points constantly in that direction.' The next day, however, when he once again started taking his daily drink containing vitamins and milk, he felt much better about his situation.

So, it was now known that there were only four competitors left: three Britons and one Frenchman, sailing two monohulls and two trimarans. And from now on, the information regarding their positions and progress became more and more scant, non-existent, or even just plain false. However, that didn't stop the sponsoring newspaper, *The Sunday Times*, from continually speculating in its understandable attempt to sensationalise this historic race.

On 1 December, for instance, the newspaper thought that Knox-Johnston must still be leading and that Moitessier was believed to be in the Australian Bight. And a week later, despite only being able to guess that Moitessier might now be crossing the Tasman Sea and that Knox-Johnston was probably somewhere between New Zealand and Cape Horn, the newspaper was confident enough to say that *Joshua* continued to make gains on *Suhaili*. As it happens, that is exactly what was happening.

The same issue of the newspaper contained more specific information regarding the two trimarans although any accuracy could only be credited to one of them. While Tetley had been in radio contact to say that he had rounded the Cape of Good Hope, from now on – unknown to the world – reports of Crowhurst's positions had to be treated with the utmost suspicion. That day *The Sunday Times* reported that *Teignmouth Electron* had covered 1,200 miles the previous week, was now about 400 miles south of the Cape Verdes and that Crowhurst was realising his potential speeds. However, two days before, on 6 December, he had begun to deliberately fake his navigation records and this would soon lead to him keeping a second logbook. In this he would continue to record his actual positions, while in his first logbook – which was barely half full – he would start to record a series of false positions with a view to implementing an extraordinary deception plan.

And the plan began in spectacular style. 'Crowhurst Speed World Record?' read *The Sunday Times* headline on 15 December. He had, apparently, sailed a record-breaking 243 miles in twenty-four hours a week earlier. Crowhurst had reported this to Hallworth on 11 December in a radio message, during which he said: 'It took a pretty strong nerve. I have never sailed so fast in all my life.' *The Sunday Times* reported that Crowhurst now thought that he had a fair chance of being the first home. To do so he would need to average 170 miles a day – assuming the sailors in front of him maintained their previous daily averages – which the newspaper thought would be possible in ideal conditions, but that it was extremely unlikely in a voyage of that length. It was thought, however, that he had a very good chance of winning the cash prize for the fastest circumnavigation, and Crowhurst himself already had an opinion on how he would like to be paid. 'I have been listening to the European money crisis on the BBC,' he said in his radio message, 'and I can tell *The Sunday Times* that if I win they can pay me in Deutschmarks.' Both Captain Craig Rich (who was advising *The Sunday Times* on navigation matters) and Sir Francis Chichester (chairman of the panel of judges) expressed scepticism regarding Crowhurst's record claim. Chichester said he must be 'a bit of a joker' and that his claims should be closely examined when he got home. And with good reason: on the day he claimed this record, Crowhurst had actually sailed 170 miles.

The same issue reported that Tetley was just over 1,000 miles east of the Cape of Good Hope and, even though there was still no news of the positions of either of the monohulls, the newspaper felt able to report that *Joshua* was gaining on *Suhaili* by an estimated 693 miles a week.

On 17 December, Crowhurst sent his first deliberately misleading telegram to Hallworth in which he said he was 'through Doldrums, over Equator' when he was still 180 miles north of the Equator. The next day, *Suhaili* was almost halfway between New Zealand and Cape Horn, and was 'bowling along under plain sail with two reefs in the main and one in the mizzen,' Knox-Johnston wrote in his log. 'This is race-winning form, if it's not too late. We're doing a comfortable six knots, I should say.'

On the same day, for the first time in two months, there was news of Moitessier, or at least for most people in the world other than Knox-Johnston.

This was when he brought *Joshua* close to the south coast of Tasmania and encountered a small fishing boat. Although he was able to give them messages which eventually got through to his wife, friends and *The Sunday Times*, he was disappointed that he didn't get any news back:

> No one could give me news of my friends. One had heard something about
> an English yachtsman who rounded New Zealand without having stopped.
> When? The fisherman did not exactly know. They seemed to remember
> the radio mentioning it last month. I do not think it is Bill King; perhaps
> it is Knox-Johnston. Of the three who set out around June, only he had a
> real sea boat. The two others sailed in little plastic things, really fragile for
> such a long trip in high latitudes. Shortly before starting I learned that one
> of them had to give up, well before Good Hope. I will listen more carefully
> to the Australian broadcasts for a few days. They might mention *Joshua*'s
> passing through their waters and give the whole picture, saying where the
> others are. But I am not kidding myself … we are alone facing infinity.

When Knox-Johnston had seen Bruce Maxwell off Otago on 21 November, he said that he expected to round Cape Horn in the first week of January and, in the absence of any further information, *The Sunday Times* used that as a basis for their ongoing reports. On 22 December, the newspaper declared that a great contest was building up for the Golden Globe, the prize for the first man home. The article did, however, include conflicting predictions: on the one hand that Knox-Johnston would be back in Falmouth on 10 April, a fortnight before Moitessier, and on the other hand Chichester was quoted as saying that Moitessier would overtake Knox-Johnston around the Falkland Islands. Meanwhile in the *Sunday Mirror*, Bruce Maxwell wrote that, having heard of Moitessier's Tasmanian encounter, he was at least two weeks further behind Knox-Johnston than previously thought. The paper also reported Crowhurst's alleged crossing of the equator, and that Tetley was making steady progress across the Indian Ocean and had sailed 185 miles in the previous twenty-four hours.

Crowhurst sent radio messages on 23 and 26 December, claiming in both that he was averaging 170 miles per day, and as a result of this *The Sunday Times* subsequently revised his estimated finishing time to the end of September, a month and a half earlier than previously thought. Rather significantly, Crowhurst gave no information regarding his position in either of these messages, but by this time the positions noted in his two logbooks differed by nearly 400 miles.

The four remaining competitors did their best to be festive on Christmas Day. Moitessier enjoyed a smoked York ham which had been specially prepared for him by Fougeron and other friends. 'I had kept it in the hold under its original wrapping,' he wrote. 'The ham is perfect without a trace of mould after four months in a humid atmosphere.' With it he had onions, garlic, camembert cheese and a tin of tomato sauce. Crowhurst enjoyed an egg and corned beef vindaloo, an orange, and some brazil nuts. Knox-Johnson made a currant duff in the morning but didn't eat it till the evening (by which time it had 'gone soggy') because he 'rather overestimated on the quantity' when preparing his lunch which consisted of stewed steak, and potatoes and peas 'cooked separately for a change'. Tetley probably ate the best meal, but then it is likely that he did so throughout his voyage thanks to the thorough preparations by his wife Eve, and he was able to enjoy a roast pheasant in mushroom sauce. During his lunch, he took a photograph of himself sitting at *Victress*'s saloon table and it appeared in *The Sunday Times* more than six weeks later under the heading: 'The Day A Solo Sailor Feels At His Loneliest'. In the photograph he is looking at the camera and raising his new pewter mug – a Christmas present from Eve which he had unwrapped that morning along with a stainless steel comb from his son – as if proposing a toast.

In the other trimaran, Crowhurst should also have had presents to unwrap, including a cuddly ventriloquist's doll with long golden hair that he could, perhaps, talk to; some cherry nougat and a book on yoga. His wife Clare had bought these items for him and even put them aboard *Teignmouth Electron* herself and laid them on his bunk in the days leading up to departure. But, in all the confusion, the bag in which they were wrapped had been mysteriously taken off the boat again and left ashore. Crowhurst did, however, have two cards from friends, one of which included the words: 'even at this stage you must feel a great sense of achievement'. Back home, Clare gave the doll to her daughter rather than let it go to waste.

All four sailors enjoyed a drink that day. Crowhurst had some brown ale; Tetley had a sherry before lunch and then enjoyed champagne (in his new pewter mug) with his meal; Moitessier also had some champagne, which had been given to him by *Joshua*'s designer; and Knox-Johnston had some whisky and wine allowing him to drink a Loyal Toast to the Queen. He wrote later:

I wish I could have heard the Queen's speech. Somehow it always adds to the charm of Christmas to gather together and listen to our hereditary ruler (or representative if you are republican minded) and think there are people all over the world doing exactly the same. For that brief time the world seems smaller. I wish it was.

Knox-Johnston reflected on the fact that, although he had spent the previous eleven Christmases at sea on British India ships, 'for the first time since I left Falmouth I felt as if I was missing something, and that perhaps it is rather stupid to spend one whole year of one's life stuck out on one's own away from all the comforts and attractions that home offers.' Inevitably he thought of his family and he recalled his mother telling him the night before he left Falmouth that he was 'totally irresponsible'. 'On this Christmas day I began to think she was right,' he wrote later. 'I was sailing round the world simply because I bloody well wanted to – and, I realised, I was thoroughly enjoying myself.'

On Christmas Eve, after a couple of glasses of whisky, Knox-Johnston had 'clambered out on deck and perched myself on the cabin top to hold a Carol Service … By the time I had exhausted my repertoire and had a few encores I was feeling quite merry.' Crowhurst's seasonal musical interlude began at daybreak on Christmas Day when he heard 'The Holly and the Ivy' by Joan Sutherland on the radio and, sponsored as he was by Music for Pleasure, Tetley was able to enjoy a recording of carols from Guildford Cathedral.

Knox-Johnston's sponsoring newspaper the *Sunday Mirror* reported on 29 December on 'the most incredible journey in the history of the world.' This was not, however, anything to do with the Golden Globe, but was about NASA's Apollo 8 space flight, the first manned mission to escape Earth's gravity and to orbit the moon. 'The three brave men who had reached for the stars' had splashed down safely in the northern Pacific Ocean two days before.

On the same day, *The Sunday Times* calculated *Suhaili's* likely finishing dated based on a comparison with *Lively Lady's* voyage a year earlier. It was thought that Knox-Johnston's speed and route were very similar to those of Sir Alec Rose, albeit about three months earlier in the year. Rose had taken 151 days from Bluff, New Zealand to home. The paper thought it was reasonable to assume that Knox-Johnston would be faster by 2 per cent, in which case he would arrive in Falmouth on about 12 April, almost a fortnight ahead of Moitessier.

'Lone Sailor Faces Vital Test,' was the headline in *The Sunday Times* on 5 January, referring to Knox-Johnston's forthcoming rounding of Cape Horn, the most legendary of headlands, although speculation with regard to the timing of this event was slightly optimistic. The paper thought that 'according to the most detailed oceanographic calculations' he would now be within 700 miles of the Cape, whereas he was actually more than 1,000 miles away at that point. Meanwhile Moitessier was estimated to be 400 miles south-east of New Zealand, Tetley was known to have been 650 miles west-south-west of Cape Leeuwin three days earlier, and Crowhurst claimed to have passed Tristan da Cunha. *Teignmouth Electron*'s actual position, however, was about 1,800 miles to the north-west but this new claim of Crowhurst's prompted the newspaper to bring forward his estimated finishing date again, to 8 September. On 8 January, Crowhurst received a telegram from Hallworth putting him in the picture with regard to his competitors: 'ROBIN LEADS – BERNARD BEYOND TASMANIA – TETLEY EASTERN INDIAN – YOUR AVERAGE DAILY 30 MILES HIGHER – SUNDAY TIMES RECKONS WINNER HOME APRIL NINE – THIS YOUR TARGET.'

Although Knox-Johnston was unable to use his radio to transmit, he was still able to receive, and on 9 January he wrote in his log:

> Just heard on the Voice of America that the Chilean Navy has been asked to look out for a 'damaged ketch' battling towards Cape Horn. The lone yachtsman, 'Me', has a lead of 3,000 miles over his nearest competitor. That's splendid news even if the lead must be down to 2,000 miles by now – still it's not lost yet and we have a fighting chance. I don't know what the damage referred to is.

The Chilean Navy's search came to nothing, however, but as the *Sunday Mirror* put it, 'this is not regarded as unusual because their chances of sighting Knox-Johnston's yacht, the small 32ft *Suhaili*, are slim.'

The optimism about the timing of *Suhaili*'s rounding of the Horn was shared by Knox-Johnston's parents who, on 10 January, had a champagne party to mark the supposed occasion.

Two days later, *The Sunday Times* updated their estimated finishing dates, although these were based on last known positions of the two monohulls which were twenty-five days (*Joshua*) and fifty-two days (*Suhaili*) earlier, and a position from *Teignmouth Electron* which was inaccurate to the tune of more than 1,000 miles (not that anyone was to know this at the time). *Suhaili* and *Joshua*'s predicted finishing dates were unchanged from earlier issues (12 and 24 April respectively) while *Victress*'s date was now 1 July, and *Teignmouth Electron*'s 26 August. This would give the Golden Globe trophy to Knox-Johnston and the £5,000 prize to Moitessier.

In the second week of January, *Victress* – when she was about 450 miles south of Cape Leeuwin – experienced some appalling weather. Tetley spent a whole day hove to while the wind blew Force 11 with gusts of Force 12. During this time, he feared for his boat, and decided that if she survived he would retire and sail in to Albany in south-west Australia. However, as it happens, *Victress* suffered remarkably little damage and so he decided to continue, at least as far as New Zealand.

Unknown to anyone other than Knox-Johnston, *Suhaili* rounded Cape Horn on 17 January. He wrote in his log:

> We've passed it!!! Spliced the main brace and broke out Aunt Aileen's fruit cake.

He then started to contemplate the remainder of his voyage:

> Cape Horn was inevitably something of a climax in the voyage. It would have been very easy to assume that once round it, the voyage was as good as over and one could relax and sail comfortably back to Falmouth. A quick look at the chart soon puts paid to this idea.

On 19 January, Crowhurst sent two brief messages to Hallworth – again mentioning the problems with the hatch in the cockpit sole – and this would be the last contact from *Teignmouth Electron* for eleven weeks. Brief though these messages were, they allowed Hallworth to combine the meagre bits of information they contained and produce a greatly exaggerated story for the press. The following weekend, *The Sunday Times* reported that Crowhurst had been in serious trouble in the Indian Ocean. An enormous wave had apparently smashed over *Teignmouth Electron,* causing a fair amount of damage that Crowhurst spent three days repairing, and he would now have to significantly reduce speed to avoid further damage. Hallworth told the newspaper that 'this mishap must be regarded as a serious handicap to his chances of putting up the fastest time in the race.' Apparently, he had been

700 miles east of the Cape of Good Hope earlier that week, whereas his true position had been about 1,000 miles east of Rio de Janeiro. The same issue said that it was not known if *Suhaili* had rounded Cape Horn, but that *Joshua* was expected to round on 9 February.

On 31 January, Sir Francis Chichester presented a Royal Institution Discourse on the subject of the Golden Globe race. He talked about the enormous difficulties facing the solo circumnavigators and he praised those who had retired:

> Some remarkably fine passages have been achieved. Captain John Ridgway and Sergeant Chay Blyth, the Atlantic rowers, both had 30ft sloops which appeared unsuitable to me: I think they did remarkably well to get as far as they did ... Ten years ago, these passages would have been reckoned as sailing feats.

He then went on to assess the chances of the four men left in the race:

> I think, judging on form, that Moitessier will be first home in the round-the-world race, and will make easily the fastest time ... I think that without his self-steering gear [Knox-Johnston] cannot be round the Horn already, though he could just have done it this weekend. If reports of his damaged gear are correct, it will be little short of a miracle if he can make Falmouth without putting in somewhere for repairs. I believe that Moitessier will be at the Horn by February 10 and that he should reach Plymouth about May 1, overtaking [Knox-Johnston] between the Falkland Islands and the Equator ... Naturally this is guessing as well as reckoning ... Lieut-Cmdr Nigel Tetley, in Victress, shows signs of being a master seaman, and there is no doubt that he has done extremely well so far. Anything can happen at sea and with remarkably good luck he could be the winner if both the leading yachts have to pull out of the race. If he succeeds I think he will reach England at the beginning of July ... Donald Crowhurst claims some fast bursts of speed including a record for the fastest day's run; but on average speeds he does not seem a likely prize-winner.

On 2 February, Tetley arrived off Otago, where Knox-Johnston had left seventy-three days earlier, and passed a package of photographs and mail to a small fishing boat. According to the New Zealand radio stations there was a hurricane forecast and so Tetley headed straight back out to sea. He would be safer there. The next day *Suhaili* officially left the Southern Ocean when she crossed the 40-degree South line of latitude.

Joshua rounded the Horn on 6 February, while *Victress* was about 560 miles east of New Zealand. Three days later, *The Sunday Times* estimated that *Teignmouth Electron* was almost halfway between the Cape of Good Hope and Cape Leeuwin, although in reality he was about 600 miles east of Buenos Aires.

Soon after *Joshua* rounded Cape Horn, Moitessier wrote in his log: 'I wonder. Plymouth so close, barely 10,000 miles to the north … Leaving from Plymouth and returning to Plymouth now seems like leaving from nowhere to go nowhere.' This was the first indication (albeit not publicly known) of another extraordinary turn that the Golden Globe race was about to take. He pressed on, however, and headed for the Falklands, as he was keen that his friends and family should know his whereabouts. He arrived there on 10 February hoping to see a vessel to which he could pass mail and photographs. However, as he was too tired to sail into Port Stanley, he hove-to outside its estuary and waited there for a while before giving up hope of seeing anyone, and then he set sail again. He had been seen, however, although not, at first, positively identified. It was only after cables were exchanged between London and the Port Stanley harbour master, with descriptions of the two yachts it was most likely to have been – *Suhaili* and *Joshua* – that it was confirmed that it was indeed the latter.

The following weekend the Sunday newspapers had a field day. 'Moitessier will break round-world record,' read the headline in *The Sunday Times*. It was estimated that on 2 March he would cross his outward track at a point in the South Atlantic that he first passed on 3 October, not that crossing an outward path was relevant to the rules of the race or to round-the-world record-breaking.

By this time, however, Moitessier had all but decided he would retire from the race and head, once more, towards the Pacific. As he sailed away from the Falklands he was exhausted, and he decided to continue sailing north-east to get away from any likelihood of encountering icebergs and also to try to get some rest. He wrote:

I let my mind heave-to for the duration … thinking about neither Plymouth nor the Pacific, not anything. Gradually the fatigue left my brain,

THE FIRST AND THE FASTEST

and the question of what route to take was no longer a question. A few more days towards the north-east to clear the iceberg zone, and I will be able to steer east toward Good Hope, Leeuwin and the Pacific.

Meanwhile the *Sunday Mirror* were showing more concern for their own man with the headline 'Where is Robin?', a question prompted by the realisation that the yacht sighted off the Falklands wasn't *Suhaili*. It was thought that she would be in the South Atlantic off the coast of Brazil and as it happens she was, albeit only just as she was almost due east of Brazil's border with Uruguay, but that did put her nearly 2,000 miles ahead of *Joshua*.
The article suggested that even Knox-Johnston's family and close friends must be wondering if he would ever be seen again.

Just over a week after passing the Falklands, on 18 February, *Joshua* crossed the 40-degree South line of latitude, altered course to starboard and headed towards Cape Town. Moitessier had come to a definite decision that he would abandon the race – and with it, albeit unknown to him at that time, the odds-on chance of the £5,000 cash prize and a good chance of the Golden Globe trophy as well – so that he could carry on sailing around the world. He later wrote by way of explanation to the race organisers:

> My intention is to continue the voyage still non-stop, towards the Pacific Islands, where there is plenty of sun and more peace than in Europe. Please do not think I am trying to break a record. 'Record' is a very stupid word at sea. I am continuing non-stop because I am happy at sea, and perhaps because I want to save my soul.

At that time, he wasn't sure whether Tahiti or Galapagos would be his final destination.

Three days after Moitessier's effective retirement, and blissfully unaware of it as was the rest of the world, Knox-Johnston had a day's run of just 18 miles which followed previous disappointing days of 40 and 36 miles. 'Does anyone wonder that I am in despair!' he wrote in his log.

'Fears Grow For Knox-Johnston,' read *The Sunday Times* headline on 23 February with still no word of him. Meanwhile the newspaper continued to assume positions for *Joshua* based on her previous daily averages and her sighting in the Falklands, and – reasonably but wrongly – assuming her continuing track towards England. It was thought that she would now be about 1,250 miles east of the River Plate and probably encountering the frustrating winds of the Doldrums. The newspaper was still estimating that he would finish on 24 April. With regard to the two trimarans, it was reported that Crowhurst hadn't been in contact and that his progress across the Indian Ocean would have been considerably slowed after the damage his boat had sustained the previous month, and that Tetley had managed to call Wellington radio three days before and was about halfway between New Zealand and Cape Horn.

On 28 February, Moitessier had a temporary change of heart: he decided to head north again and return to Europe. Although he had been planning to head for Cape Town with a view to passing on his news to another vessel, he was all too aware of the difficulties and unreliability of doing so. Getting to the finish line, however, would be a guaranteed way of letting his family and friends know that he was alright. And there seemed to be many other compelling reasons to head for Plymouth: he had just been through another gale which tired him out and made him wonder if he wanted to spend too much more time at sea, particularly crossing the Indian Ocean again; he wanted to see his mother; the wind had shifted to the north-east which he thought was 'a sign'; he wanted to collect all the gear that he had left behind when reducing *Joshua*'s weight; and he had ninety-two 100ft rolls of film which he wanted to deliver safely before they were spoilt. 'There are so many things in those images,' he wrote, 'so many true things I would like to share with others.'

Over the next couple of days, the matter continued to bother him considerably. He began to think that the best thing might be to call at St Helena or Ascension Island to get a message through to his family, but at the same time he doubted his own likely actions:

> I wouldn't have stopped. I would have pushed on in the trade winds telling myself 'Don't be a fool, you may as well just put in a little effort, try to pick up *The Sunday Times* prize and leave again right away ...' I know how it goes.

And so he changed his mind for a third and final time, and once more altered course to starboard and headed for Cape Town, writing that he 'felt physically sick at the thought of getting back to Europe. Back to the snake pit.'

But still no one knew about any of these changes, of course, and *The Sunday Times* continued to assume he was on his way home. On 2 March the newspaper estimated he was about 650 miles south-east of Trinidade Island and that he was expected to cross his outward track in the South Atlantic that weekend, thus becoming the fastest – and possibly the first – non-stop circumnavigator. The word 'possibly' was used as there was still no news of Knox-Johnston, but it was thought that there was a possibility that he might have rounded Cape Horn and sailed into the South Atlantic unseen. Five days earlier, Tetley had reported that he was just over 2,000 miles from Cape Horn while Crowhurst was thought to be approaching Cape Leeuwin.

During this time, *Victress* – about as far from civilisation as it is possible to be – was experiencing horrendous conditions. On 26 February, she had been caught by a rogue wave which caused her to heel over to about 55 degrees. Monohulls frequently heel over at this sort of angle, but for a multihull it could be beyond the point of no return. Somehow, however, *Victress* came upright again and pressed on. Six days later, she was hit by another rogue wave, and this one stove in a large saloon window allowing gallons of water to pour into the main hull, completely soaking everything in sight, including Tetley himself. He worked furiously to save his boat, and himself, first by bailing out the water – with a bucket because the bilge pump had become clogged up – and then by fixing a piece of plywood over the gaping hole where the window had been, all the while praying that another wave wouldn't follow the first one. The next morning, during a thorough inspection of *Victress* he found a number of serious structural issues in two of the hulls. His immediate reaction was that now was the time to retire from the race and head for port, Valparaiso in Chile seeming the best bet. But the next day things didn't seem so bad – the weather had cleared up a bit and he had restored some order to his devastated cabin – and he changed his mind. After all, Valparaiso was no nearer than the Horn, and once he was back in the Atlantic things would surely be easier.

Tetley wasn't the only trimaran skipper contemplating calling in at a South American port around this time. Crowhurst, however, went one better: he actually did so. On 6 March, *Teignmouth Electron* crept into the River Plate Estuary, which divides Buenos Aires and Montevideo, the capital cities of Argentina and Uruguay. For weeks he had been sailing along, very slowly, off the east coast of South America, essentially killing time. But one particular problem on *Teignmouth Electron* which was becoming a major cause for concern was a split in the starboard float. The repairs that were needed would be simple enough to carry out if only he had some suitable materials. There should have been some on board, but they had been inadvertently left ashore during the chaotic preparations in Teignmouth. However, for fear of detection – not only was he about to break the 'outside assistance' rule, he was also a very long way away from where the world thought he was – he had no intention of going anywhere near the big cities. Instead he anchored off the small Argentinian town of Rio Salado. A couple of hours later three men – including the Senior Petty Officer of the small coastguard station – came out to him in a fishing boat. Crowhurst found he had no common language with them but he managed to indicate the repairs he needed to make, and they towed *Teignmouth Electron* into the river and moored her against a jetty. One of them then drove Crowhurst 17 miles along the coast to meet a French family who were able to interpret. Now that his Argentinian host understood what Crowhurst wanted, he was able to drive him back to Rio Salado where the materials were obtainable. The next day Crowhurst carried out his repairs essentially just by screwing two 18in square plywood patches to the side of the float. That evening he dined with two of his Argentinian hosts, although the conversation was, inevitably, almost non-existent. The next day, 8 March, *Teignmouth Electron* was towed back out of the river and Crowhurst set sail again. But he had chosen his port of call well. No one that he met had heard of any round the world race, and the area was so remote, and with such poor communications, that no word of his visit ever got out.

Suhaili crossed the Equator on 9 March, and Knox-Johnston 'found some spare time on my hands to prepare her, and me, for our confrontation with civilisation'. He cut his hair, trimmed his beard and the weed on *Suhaili's* hull, serviced the rigging, did some sail repairs and had a general clean up. Having seen just one ship since leaving New Zealand – a Japanese bulk carrier en route from the Cape of Good Hope to Rio de Janeiro – he was now approaching some shipping lanes and hoped to make contact with a ship that could report his position.

That same day the *Sunday Mirror* published an interview with Sir Alec Rose with the headline 'Robin Can Make It'. Rose expressed concerns about the condition of *Suhaili* – partly based on what he had heard from reports of Knox-Johnston's meeting with Bruce Maxwell in New Zealand, and partly from his assumptions about the weather she would subsequently have encountered – and pointed out how much his own boat, *Lively Lady*, had benefitted from repairs during the two stopovers in his circumnavigation. But, he said, it was too soon to write off his chances, as there was not necessarily any significance in the fact that Moitessier had been sighted only once and Knox-Johnston not at all since they left New Zealand waters. Rose rightly pointed out that even though they might have crossed busy shipping routes, 'it's a very big sea out there.'

Meanwhile, *The Sunday Times* continued to assume good progress up the Atlantic for *Joshua*: 'Moitessier On The Last Stretch' read the headline. It was thought that he would now be about 700 miles west-south-west of St Helena and that he might be sighted off the Azores in early April.

On 14 March, Tetley made his first radio contact for three weeks and reported that he was about 550 miles from Cape Horn. This was the only definite news *The Sunday Times* was able to report two days later, although the paper speculated on the positions of two other competitors: Moitessier (now the paper's favourite for both the Golden Globe trophy and the £5,000 prize) about 400 miles south of the Equator; and Crowhurst in the Australian Bight, 900 miles from Melbourne.

News of Moitessier's retirement broke on 18 March when he arrived off Cape Town. The first vessel he encountered was the BP tanker *British Argosy* whose captain, Ronald Friendship, was particularly surprised:

> When I saw the *Joshua* approaching, I was amazed because I thought Moitessier was already crossing the Equator. He catapulted a message on board and then headed southwards. He looked as fit as a fiddle, though we didn't get close enough to talk.

Joshua then sailed in to Cape Town harbour where Moitessier encountered the port captain's launch. He asked for news of his competitors but the only response he got was that 'four have been wiped out, but does not know their names,' Moitessier later wrote. 'Anything about a trimaran? He does not know.' He handed over a packet of letters in a 3-gallon jerrycan containing cassettes, ten of his reels of 16mm colour movie film, and 'two good handfuls of stills' which included photos of the logbook. 'If anything happened to me my publisher would then have all the material for writing the book in my place, and my family would be safe about my future,' he wrote.

Bizarrely, he made a point of warning the launch's crew not to come too close as he didn't want to break the Golden Globe rules. This prompted *The Sunday Times*, the following weekend, to speculate on the possibility of Moitessier re-joining the race and the fact that he could still win it. At an average of 130 miles a day, he could be back in Plymouth by 27 May, while Tetley was not expected home until 6 June. But it was all too late because Moitessier, as soon as he left Cape Town, headed towards the Pacific. In the *Sunday Mirror*, Sir Francis Chichester expressed some empathy for Moitessier's decision – 'On these long voyages, you develop a sort of rhythm of life with the boat and the sea,' he said, 'and you are very loth to break that rhythm.' And much later, in a conversation with Knox-Johnston after *Suhaili* had arrived back in Falmouth, he expressed further views:

> The whole thing was quite incomprehensible, though the strange thing is that the same impulse had occurred to me. Having got round the Horn once, I thought, 'oh let's go round again'. Then I said to myself, 'don't be so bloody stupid'.

On the same day that Moitessier called into Cape Town, *Victress* rounded Cape Horn, the first multihull ever to do so. Nigel Tetley's status in the race had now escalated dramatically: after Moitessier's retirement, and with no news of Knox-Johnston or Crowhurst, he was now favourite for both prizes. Tetley himself would not hear the news about Moitessier's retirement and his own new position as favourite until he made a radio call a week later.

During that eventful third week in March, Knox-Johnston's sponsors, the *Sunday Mirror*, began to organise a massive search for *Suhaili* involving British, Portuguese and American ships and planes. It so happened that a NATO fleet of thirty ships, eight of which were British, had recently left Lisbon for an exercise near the Cape Verde Islands and not far from Knox-Johnston's expected route, and these ships had been requested to look out for *Suhaili*. Furthermore, the *Sunday Mirror*'s reporter Bruce Maxwell was in the Azores making other arrangements. There was, and still is, a US Air Force base on Terceira island and from there long-range aircraft made daily patrols into the Atlantic – they, too, were asked to keep a look out. Also, Maxwell made a ten-minute radio broadcast from a Portuguese radio station explaining the need for the search, and this was heard by thousands of local people who alerted scores of fishing boats and other ships in the area.

The Sunday Mirror reported that it would be the biggest search ever made for any small boat, while *The Sunday Times* pointed out that, if he was spotted there soon, he would be favourite to win the Golden Globe for the first to finish, although his slow passage would rule him out of the £5,000 prize for the fastest voyage.

After leaving Rio Salado, *Teignmouth Electron* spent three weeks sailing in a generally southerly direction and, on 29 March, arrived off the Falklands. This allowed Crowhurst to take some cine film footage of a sunset over the islands – he may have needed to prove that he had sailed past them – before heading north again the following day.

'Hunt For Solo Yachtsman Is Stepped Up,' read the headline in the *Sunday Mirror* on 30 March. The paper was optimistic about the possible success of the massive air and sea search for *Suhaili* because on his outward passage Knox-Johnston had passed between the islands of Terceira and Sao Miguel to make a check on his position, and it was thought that it would be logical for him to do the same thing again.

But this time he passed well to the west of the Azores, out of range of the search party, and so still he escaped unnoticed. He did see a few ships himself though: the first, which ignored his signals, just north of the Equator on 10 March; several more over the subsequent days; and the Norwegian cargo ship on 2 April. The last of these was the first to even appear to notice him, but still didn't properly acknowledge his signals.

But at last, on 5 April, 135 days after he left Bruce Maxwell in New Zealand, he was able to make some contact with other human beings. The tanker *Mobil Acme* – which had left the Thames on 31 March bound for Beaumont in Texas – passed close enough to *Suhaili* for the two vessels to exchange signals. They were about 250 miles west of Horta. A couple of hours later, the news was out. 'They All Thought He Was Dead,' declared the *Sunday Mirror*'s headline the next day. Bruce Maxwell wrote that the Knox-Johnston family was watching *Frenchman's Creek* on TV when they heard the news, while *The Sunday Times* re-evaluated the likely prize winners: Knox-Johnston was now almost certain to win the Golden Globe, while Tetley – who had radioed Buenos Aires from a position about 750 miles east of the Argentine capital and said that he was making good progress three days earlier – was still the favourite for the £5,000 prize.

Two days later, on 7 April, Knox-Johnston saw land for the first time since Cape Horn: it was Flores and Cervo, outcrops of the Azores.

On 10 April, another trimaran skipper made contact with Buenos Aires. This time it was Crowhurst – from whom no one had heard since 18 January – who was supposedly calling from the opposite side of the South American continent to Tetley. True to form his telegram didn't give an actual position, but said 'HEADING DIGGER RAMREZ LOG KAPUT 17697'. Hallworth interpreted 'Digger Ramrez' to be Diego Ramrez, the islands off Cape Horn and somehow from this scant information he and *The Sunday Times* deduced that *Teignmouth Electron* would be rounding the famous headland on 13 April (the date the next issue of the paper was published) which was about a week earlier than Crowhurst had planned to claim he was rounding it.

'Battle Hots Up For Yacht Race Prizes,' read the headline. It was now thought that if Crowhurst could keep up his apparent average speed, his elapsed time for the voyage would be about ten days quicker than Tetley's and this would give him the £5,000 cash prize. Just over a week earlier, it looked as if Tetley would win both prizes but he now looked an unlikely bet for either. That same day, Hallworth sent Crowhurst an encouraging telegram: 'YOU'RE ONLY TWO WEEKS BEHIND TETLEY—PHOTO FINISH—WILL MAKE GREAT NEWS STOP ROBIN DUE ONE TO TWO WEEKS.' In reality, Crowhurst was about 400 miles south-east of Buenos Aires that day, having still not left the Atlantic Ocean.

The Sunday Times now thought that Knox-Johnston would arrive in Falmouth between 19 and 24 April, and so clinch the Golden Globe trophy by some margin. Chichester's own prediction was a little more precise. He thought *Suhaili* would get home on 21 April, which he thought would be a tremendous achievement, and he expressed admiration for Knox-Johnston with regard to the way he kept going despite so many problems with breakages and so on.

Knox-Johnston was still unaware of the situation with regard to Moitessier or any of his other competitors – just as Tetley hadn't heard about *Suhaili's* sighting and the radio call from Crowhurst – and he would have to wait until his conversation with the crew of the *Mungo* on 12 April before he heard anything about them. Even then, he couldn't help but be sceptical about a French crew reporting the apparently unbelievable news about their compatriot, and it wasn't until he spoke to his brother the next day that he knew it was true.

Tetley became aware of the news regarding Knox-Johnston and Crowhurst – and therefore his own considerably downgraded situation regarding the odds for both prizes – on 17 April, when he was about ten days south of the Equator. He was pleased to hear that both men were safe and not at all sorry that Knox-Johnston was destined for the Golden Globe trophy, but he was somewhat riled by the prospect of another trimaran completing the voyage in a faster elapsed time than *Victress*. He had, for some time and to some extent, been nursing his increasingly frail boat along, but now things had changed and he needed to push on.

On 18 April, Portishead radio sent Crowhurst a message informing him of Moitessier's retirement and Tetley's current position. The following day, Knox-Johnston was 150 miles south-west of the Isles of Scilly in a worsening gale with 18ft waves. He radioed that *Suhaili* had taken a bit of a bashing and that he had had only one hour's sleep the previous night. The wind was from the wrong direction to get him home easily and Knox-Johnston was hove-to under bare poles and streaming a warp. He later wrote:

> I was tired and depressed. There was nothing I could do until the wind changed or eased and I turned in. This was the limit: to come this far and then get a contrary gale just when I could almost smell home, was too much.

Meanwhile, the two trimarans were both now in the South Atlantic. Actually, they had been ever since *Victress* rounded the Horn on 18 March, at which point *Teignmouth Electron* was less than 100 miles from the coast of Argentina and about 600 miles north of the Falklands. Furthermore, during the following week their paths converged (while Crowhurst was sailing south) until they probably passed extremely close to each other in a position about 80 miles north of the Falklands. But Crowhurst was now also *officially* in the South Atlantic – *The Sunday Times* reported his position as about halfway between Cape Horn and the Falklands – while Tetley was about 300 miles east of the Brazilian city of Salvador.

The conditions gradually eased for Knox-Johnston, and in the early hours of 21 April the wind went round to the south-west, at last allowing him to sail in the direction he needed to go. By dawn the following day he had passed the Lizard – the most southerly point of mainland Britain – and was sailing nicely towards Falmouth. However, at about 9 a.m., when *Suhaili* was just 6 miles from her finishing line, the wind swung round to the north-north-west – pretty much on the nose – and increased to a Force 7 to 8. The two hours or so that he thought it would take him to get home turned into more than six but eventually, at 3.25 p.m., one of the most significant voyages in maritime history came to an end.

As it happens a second, by no means insignificant, maritime event occurred on the very same day. *Victress*, in a position about 300 miles east-north-east of Recife, crossed her outward path and therefore became the first trimaran to complete a geographical circumnavigation of the world. She nearly didn't, however, because two days earlier, when only 60 miles from this position, Tetley had almost given up. *Victress* was in a bad way and, although he was realistic enough to accept that she would be a write-off by the end of the voyage, he just had to get her home. But instead of sailing her gently, the knowledge of Crowhurst catching him up and threatening to beat him in terms of elapsed time, forced him to push her harder than he knew he should. On 20 April, however, further inspection of *Victress* persuaded Tetley that the right thing to do was to retire from the race and head for Recife. But he needed to make some repairs before doing so, and so he set to work. He spent two days patching things up and he found himself making a much better job than he expected. A couple of days of reflection on such decision-making can also change things and so, with new life breathed into *Victress*, he pointed her bows, once more, towards Plymouth which was 4,200 miles away.

With no further definite news on the positions of the trimarans, on 27 April *The Sunday Times* reported that *Victress* was estimated to be just over 600 miles north of the north-east tip of Brazil, and *Teignmouth Electron* about 600 miles north-north-east of the Falklands.

Crowhurst sent two telegrams on 30 April. In one, to the BBC, he sent his congratulations to Robin Knox-Johnston, while adding: 'BUT KINDLY NOTE NOT RACE WINNER YET'. The other was to Hallworth, who then passed on the contents to *The Sunday Times*:

181 days after departing Lizard, I have seen my first land, the Falklands. I hove-to for almost an hour, filming and watching the sundown. Hazy autumn evening with wood smoke on the wind, Then pell-mell for the safety of the South Atlantic.

That same day, Crowhurst effectively re-joined the race in the sense that, from then on, his declared positions coincided with his real ones, and he started to sail purposefully back up the Atlantic.

On 18 May, *The Sunday Times* reported on a radio call from Tetley the previous week. It started with a description of a new problem, that of his depleted stores, although that was by no means a serious issue. But there was also a reference to the condition of his boat: although he was having to nurse *Victress* along with a damaged bow, he was confident that she would hold together and that he would make it home. His estimated position was about 150 miles south of the Azores and he was expected to arrive in Plymouth around 2 June. Crowhurst, meanwhile, was still expected to have an elapsed time about ten days quicker than Tetley.

But just two days after these words were published, Tetley's optimism proved unfounded and his hopes were cruelly ended. He was about 130 miles north of the Azores and 1,200 miles from Plymouth when, on the night of 20 May, the wind increased to a Force 9. After all that she had been through, this proved to be the final straw for *Victress*. First the bow of her port hull broke off. This in itself may not have been catastrophic, as there was still a bulkhead at the forward end of the remaining part of the hull which would keep the worst of the sea out, but the detached section then smashed a hole in the main hull and water began to flood in. Tetley knew that he would have to abandon ship. He broadcast a Mayday call on the radio and this was immediately picked up by a Dutch vessel which was unable to come to his rescue but at least gave him some reassurance. But he had no time to lose, as *Victress* was taking in water fast. He dragged the life raft on deck and threw it in to the sea, where it inflated automatically. He climbed into it, cast himself adrift and soon afterwards lost sight of *Victress* forever.

During the night, he tried to send further distress messages with his emergency transmitter but with no response. After sunrise, he realised he hadn't been using the transmitter correctly and so he tried again. As a result of his initial contact with the Dutch ship, an American plane had been looking for him, and he was soon able to make contact with its crew. By midday a US Hercules based in the Azores had found him and, at 5.40 p.m., an Italian tanker called *Pampero* – on passage to Trinidad – rescued him.

All the attention was now on Crowhurst, as he must have realised when he heard about *Victress*'s sinking and Tetley's subsequent rescue in a telegram from his wife Clare on 23 May. 'Donald Crowhurst – The Last Of The Nine' read *The Sunday Times* headline on 25 May. At that time Crowhurst was thought to be about 750 miles south-east of Recife. Over the following weekends, *The Sunday Times's* headlines and reports continued to tell the story of *Teignmouth Electron's* apparent progress towards home. 'Crowhurst crosses Equator' on 8 June; ; 'Crowhurst Nears Home – And £5,000,' on 15 June, when Hallworth told the paper that Crowhurst now seemed to be having very little trouble with his boat; 'Crowhurst Now Just Two Weeks From Home,' on 22 June, when he was estimated to be 600 miles south-west of the Azores and when, in Teignmouth, it was reported that arrangements were being made for a huge welcome with souvenir postcards on sale and the Post Office arranging a special frank on any mail leaving Teignmouth on the day of his arrival; and 'Crowhurst Becalmed Off Azores' on 6 July. His predicted finishing date had steadily been put back and the newspaper now said that he wasn't expected before 14 July, or even later if he didn't get favourable winds. The article explained that *Teignmouth Electron* was at the centre of a large high-pressure system with almost no wind, but that he still had plenty of time – sixty-three days – to cover the last 900 miles and win the £5,000 prize for the fastest circumnavigation. And there was more news of the welcome being prepared for his homecoming: the Teign Corinthian Yacht Club had arranged for a gun salute to mark the end of his voyage, and he would be escorted home by a Royal Navy minesweeper.

Meanwhile, Crowhurst was getting some idea of the scale of the welcome that awaited him in telegrams from home: 'CONGRATULATIONS ON PROGRESS—HAVE NETWORK TELEVISION PROGRAMME FOR DAY OF YOUR RETURN,' from the BBC on 18 June, for instance; and 'BBC AND EXPRESS MEETING YOU WITH CLARE AND ME OFF SCILLIES—YOUR TRIUMPH BRINGING ONE HUNDRED THOUSAND FOLK TEIGNMOUTH WHERE FUND NOW REACHING FIFTEEN HUNDRED PLUS MANY OTHER BENEFITS,' from Hallworth on 26 June.

But Sir Francis Chichester, chairman of the panel of judges who had been sceptical about Crowhurst's apparent progress for some time, had now taken action. On 23 June, while on holiday in Portugal, he wrote to Robert Riddell *The Sunday Times* race secretary. He said that, although they shouldn't hold up his award for any longer than necessary, he felt that a rapid investigation was required as soon as *Teignmouth Electron* arrived home to check the validity of her voyage, as it might save subsequent embarrassment.

Meanwhile, Bernard Moitessier had completed his own extraordinary voyage. On 21 June, he dropped anchor at Papeete in Tahiti, 303 days after leaving Plymouth and having sailed 35,500 miles – 6,000 further than Robin Knox-Johnston. *The Sunday Times* reported that he had been pursuing his own private epic voyage, according to his own rules and that he was in fine physical condition. Bizarrely, however, he had, until he made his landfall, been complying with the Golden Globe rules and it was only now, the newspaper said, that 'he must officially – and regretfully – be removed from the lists'.

Teignmouth Electron was sighted by a ship – the Norwegian cargo vessel *Cuyahoga* – on 25 June, when she was about 750 miles south-west of the Azores. The ship's captain later reported that Crowhurst waved and seemed in good shape. Three days later, Crowhurst had his very last radio contact with anyone.

The final drama in this extraordinary Golden Globe race began to emerge on 10 July. The Royal Mail Vessel *Picardy* was on her way from London to Santo Domingo in the Caribbean when her crew sighted a small sailing vessel. It was *Teignmouth Electron* with just her mizzen sail up and, as it soon became apparent, no one on board. Crowhurst, it seemed, had fallen overboard. Picardy hoisted the trimaran on board and resumed her passage towards the West Indies. Three days later *The Sunday Times* announced that it was launching an appeal fund for Crowhurst's widow and four young children. It was reported that Knox-Johnston, who was now the beneficiary of the £5,000 prize for the fastest time as well as the winner of the Golden Globe, had generously announced that he would be donating this money to the appeal fund. He said:

> I am greatly upset at the news, all the more because Donald Crowhurst was almost certain to make the fastest time. In the circumstances, I would not want to accept the £5,000 and I have asked for the money to go towards setting up a fund for Mrs Crowhurst and her four children.

'It is very sad that such an extraordinary accident should have occurred to such a gallant sailor after such a memorable voyage, and so near home,' said Sir Francis Chichester. 'But before he was lost, he had accomplished something near to his heart, having circumnavigated the world.'

But soon afterwards, events took another dramatic turn. *The Sunday Times* journalist Nicholas Tomalin flew out to Santo Domingo with Hallworth and a photographer to examine *Teignmouth Electron* after the Picardy had delivered her there on 16 July. They found on board Crowhurst's logbooks, and during the course of the next day they discovered his great deception: that he had never left the Atlantic Ocean. Tomalin took the logbooks back to London where they were 'carefully and expertly commented on by a navigator and a psychiatrist,' he later wrote. 'They shed an unexpected and tragic new light on the circumstances of Crowhurst's voyage and presumed death.'

This 'new light' prompted *The Sunday Times* to issue a statement 'with great sadness'. After Crowhurst's log had been examined, the statement said, it became clear that he would not have qualified for any prize even if he had returned safely to England, as *Teignmouth Electron* had never left the Atlantic; some of the radio messages Crowhurst had sent had been misleading; and he was under considerable mental strain towards the end of his voyage.

'The logbooks reveal Donald Crowhurst as a man of great courage and determination,' continued Tomalin, 'who took on a challenge so immense that, in some ways that can probably never be finally established, it destroyed him … the logs indicate that the loneliness, danger and progressive breakup of his boat threatened – at times – his mental balance.' Tomalin wrote that it would always be a mystery as to whether his false radio messages were deliberately intended to deceive or whether they were sent in 'a state of mental stress', and that 'he also clearly indicated that he wanted the world to know precisely what had happened on the voyage.'

In the light of this new information, *The Sunday Times* insisted that Knox-Johnston should accept the £5,000 prize money. This he did, but with no intention of keeping it. He said:

> Long distance sailors will realise the strain that Donald Crowhurst must have undergone. None of us should judge him harshly. With the feeling that we should respect the dead and care for the living, I still wish to donate *The Sunday Times* prize to Mrs Crowhurst to help with the bringing up of her four young children.

Sir Francis Chichester said that he had had his suspicions about Crowhurst's voyage, based on the dearth of radio messages for eleven weeks (he thought this was strange, considering that he was an electronics engineer), the fact that he hadn't been sighted anywhere along the 12,500-mile stretch of the Southern Ocean, and because of his various puzzling statements. He said that, as chairman of the Golden Globe race judges, he had decided some time previously that Crowhurst's log should be thoroughly scrutinised.

So if Moitessier had returned to Plymouth he would, almost without doubt, have been awarded the prize for the fastest circumnavigation. But would he have won the Golden Globe Trophy for the first? Throughout the race *The Sunday Times,* in particular, had fostered speculation on the issue and had suggested it would be a close finish, but that is hardly surprising as they wanted to sell newspapers. Knox-Johnston wrote, quite rightly, that it was impossible to say who would have been first home. *Joshua* was sighted off the Falklands eighteen days after *Suhaili* had passed there and, on that day, 10 February, the smaller boat was in the variables and had slowed down, as would *Joshua* have done when she reached there. But even, Knox-Johnston calculated, if *Joshua* had kept up her full average speed of 117 miles per day all the way home, the Frenchman would still have been 50 miles away from Plymouth on the day *Suhaili* arrived in Falmouth. 'This may satisfy a mathematician,' Knox-Johnston wrote later, 'but no seaman would be so foolish as to say who would have been first. There are too many imponderables at sea.'

In the conversation between Francis Chichester and Knox-Johnston that was published in *The Sunday Times* on 27 April 1969, Chichester voiced his own opinions on the subject. He had worked out that, if Moitessier had kept up the average speed he had achieved up to Cape Horn all the way to Plymouth, he would have won by two and a quarter days. 'But since that is 8,800 miles away it is ridiculous to say he had it in the bag,' he said.

And what did Moitessier himself think? Well, he is known to have written about the issue on three occasions: to correct an American magazine which had wrongly reported that he was actually leading when he pulled out; in his book *The Long Way* in which he said that 'it is by no means certain that *Joshua* would have finished first' and that, if she had, 'it would have been a grave injustice as Knox-Johnston's boat was much smaller, and much less sound'; and in a letter to Knox-Johnston himself to say that he didn't think that *Joshua* would have won.

MacArthur's Voyage

For almost all the of time that Knox-Johnston was making his way down the Atlantic in the early part of his circumnavigation, he could only really think about the two competitors who had started a week and two weeks before him. But, by the time Blyth and Ridgway had retired, four boats which he knew would be considerably faster than *Suhaili* had started – and two more were still to start – and he turned his attention to them, or at least as much as the sporadic communications allowed him to. It was far from a conventional race, but the script could hardly have been better written, with the slow boats starting first and the faster ones after the right sort of interlude to foster predictions of close finishes.

MacArthur's race was equally unconventional. But whereas Knox-Johnston had, at various times, eight competitors, she had just one, although there could be different points of view as to who or what that competitor was: Francis Joyon or the clock. At different times MacArthur herself looked at it both ways. In her log and emails she often referred to the clock and the fact that it was 'always ticking' and at another time she wrote that it felt as if Joyon was out on the same part of the ocean as she was.

Chasing an existing record is fundamentally different to taking part in a conventional race in which all the competitors start from the same place at the same time. MacArthur often compared her own situation with that of races such as the Vendée Globe in which she had competed four years earlier. She wrote about the fact that, in a conventional race, a boat in front of her might encounter adverse conditions such as light airs, or may not even make it to the finish for some reason. But she was all too aware that, in this case, she was racing against a record that was 'set in stone', and against a 'totally indestructible, infallible pace boat which had finished its journey'. Every time she fell behind the record pace, her subsequent average speeds would simply have to increase, and with that there would be more potential danger.

•—◆—•

B&Q crossed the Lizard–Ushant start line at 27 knots at 0810 on 28 November 2004. 'MacArthur Relieved To Start Record Attempt,' read the headline in the next day's *The Daily Telegraph,* which then reported that:

> [The] first 151 miles were dashed off at the very speed MacArthur needs to average for the voyage, at least 16 knots. She was straight in to heart-on-sleeve-mode. 'Relief to have started … I was so nervous and very emotional,' she said.

Despite sailing 548 miles in the first thirty-one hours and achieving a twenty-four-hour run of 414.3 miles on day two, *B&Q* was almost two hours behind the record at the end of that day. But over the next few days she pulled slightly ahead, before falling two and a half hours behind again on day six. Again, things improved until she was almost half a day ahead when she crossed the Equator in a record solo time of eight days and 18 hours.

Just before she entered the southern hemisphere, she encountered two Royal Navy ships: the Royal Fleet Auxiliary *Gold Rover* and HMS *Iron Duke*. They stayed with her for about an hour, during which they sent a helicopter over to 'buzz' *B&Q* and MacArthur had radio conversations with the helicopter crew and *Iron Duke*'s captain. 'I felt really emotional once they had gone,' she later wrote.

Sailing through the Doldrums, the winds fluctuated rapidly between 5 and 20 knots and she wrote of the multiple sail changes these conditions forced her to make, but she did concede that *B&Q* got through the area more easily than she might have done.

On day ten, she was already anticipating the Southern Ocean about which she was apprehensive but at the same time looking forward to its challenges. On day fourteen she was over a day ahead for the first time, but over the following three days she slipped back until her lead was just over four hours. But the next day – thanks to her best day's run so far, 488.4 miles – she was, once more, over half a day ahead. She was now just over a thousand miles south-west of the Cape of Good Hope and, although it was getting distinctly colder, she was finding that she preferred that to the heat of the Equator.

She set another record when she passed the longitude of the Cape of Good Hope after 19 days 9 hours 46 minutes. On day twenty-two, she was, once again, but briefly, over a day ahead but then slipped back until – on day twenty-seven, when she was 1,360 miles north-east of the Kerguelan Islands – she was less than four hours ahead. The next day – Christmas Day and 'just another day, albeit a bad one, in the office' – the lead started to build again until it was over a day on day thirty, when she passed south of Cape Leeuwin in another record time and, three days later, more than two and a half days. On day thirty-four she had another great twenty-four-hour run – 484.5 miles.

B&Q was by no means the only boat racing around the world at that time. In fact, on 2 January, MacArthur's thirty-sixth day at sea, a seriously ill crew member sailing on the Challenge 72 *Imagine It. Done* in the Global Challenge race was airlifted off the boat by a helicopter based in the Chatham Islands; and two days later, fellow British single-hander Mike Golding rounded Cape Horn in third place in the Vendée Globe.

On day forty, *B&Q* was more than three days ahead of the record for the first time and, the following day, more than four days ahead. MacArthur was delighted by this but at the same time she was all too aware that there was still a long way to go.

She then had a twenty-four-hour run of 501.6 miles which increased her lead to almost five days. This, she thought, would allow her to stop pushing the boat so hard and to take fewer risks, but at the same time she recognised that there was still a long way to go and any unforeseen circumstances could lose her time.

On day forty-five, MacArthur achieved the maximum lead of the whole voyage: eight minutes more than five days.

B&Q rounded Cape Horn the next day, setting yet another single-handed record, and continued to maintain a lead of over four days. However, light winds and head winds with big seas now began to erode that lead.

As she passed about 70 miles west of the Falkland Islands on day forty-seven, B&Q was escorted by the Royal Navy ship HMS Gloucester for about three hours, and MacArthur was treated to an air show by the ship's Lynx helicopter and by a VC10, a Hercules C130 and two Tornados from the Falklands. She was thrilled that they had made the effort to do this.

On day fifty-one, in difficult changeable weather conditions and with the lead now less than four days, MacArthur gybed B&Q nine times in one and a half hours. More difficult conditions followed until the lead was less than three days on day fifty-four, less than two the following day (the day that B&Q's homeward path crossed her outward one), and just thirteen hours on day fifty-seven. She recalled how Francis Joyon hadn't had the best of voyages in the South Atlantic either but felt that hers was even worse. She experienced mixed emotions on day fifty-four when she passed another Royal Navy ship, HMS Endurance which was on her way south. While she was delighted to pass close enough to the ship to witness the enthusiastic support of her crew, her morale quickly deteriorated as soon as they were gone and she got back to focusing on the precarious situation with regard to her record attempt.

Looking at the conditions ahead of her, MacArthur was now anticipating that B&Q would be behind the record by the time she reached the Equator, but she was a long way from giving up. She decided that it would be better not to think about the significant lead she had previously had, but just to focus on her present situation.

On day fifty-eight, when she was little more than 1,000 miles from the Equator, B&Q was all but level with the record. MacArthur was very philosophical about losing the substantial lead she had previously had, recognising that if she hadn't had that lead she would now be a long way behind the record rather than level with it.

That same day, the catamaran *Orange II* crossed the Lizard–Ushant starting line at the beginning of a Jules Verne attempt which would end successfully, with the record broken by almost thirteen days.

That night the breeze dropped to just 4 knots and the following day *B&Q* was behind the record – for the first time for more than seven weeks – by ten hours. Again MacArthur remained positive, recognising that she didn't need to beat the record by anything other than the smallest of margins. But the deficit was short-lived, as *B&Q* was ahead again on day sixty – albeit by just six hours – and from then MacArthur managed to rebuild her lead so that her earlier prediction regarding the situation when crossing the Equator proved to be wrong. By then, on day sixty-one, *B&Q* was over a day ahead and so completed a clean sweep of records at all the intermediate natural milestones: crossing the Equator in both directions and passing south of the three Great Capes. While crossing the Equator this time, in the time-honoured tradition of sailors, MacArthur gave Neptune a gift, in this case a silver necklace: 'the most precious thing I had to give to get us home!'

On day sixty-three *B&Q*'s lead was almost a day and a half and, although MacArthur was turning her thoughts to the finish line, she was 'petrified' that she wouldn't make it there in time. But the lead continued to build until it was nearly three and a half days on day sixty-seven (when, incidentally, Vincent Riou arrived in Les Sables d'Olonne to win the Vendée Globe race), and then it started to fall again: 3 days 6 hours on day sixty-eight, 2 days 13 hours on day sixty-nine, 2 days 6 hours on day seventy, 1 day 23 hours on day seventy-one. That day, MacArthur encountered yet another Royal Navy ship, the Type 42 destroyer HMS *Liverpool*, and she too sent up a helicopter to 'buzz' *B&Q*. Around the same time, a light aircraft from Spain and an RAF Nimrod flew overhead, promoting MacArthur to write that she 'needed air traffic control out here!'

Finally, the next night, with the lead reduced still further to 1 day 8 hours 35 minutes 49 seconds, *B&Q* crossed the Lizard–Ushant finishing line. After days of really difficult and changeable weather conditions, eventually things had gone her way, and when they did she felt 'utter joy'

B&Q sailed a total of 27,354 miles during her record-breaking circumnavigation, at an average speed of 15.9 knots. MacArthur later discovered that her voyage time of 71 days 14 hours 18 minutes 33 seconds was faster – albeit by was less than six minutes – than the fully-crewed round-the-world record just over three years earlier.

10

Homecomings

'WORLD BEATER ROBIN – WE GREET OUR LONE SAILOR ON LAST LAP,' read the headline on the front page of the *Daily Mirror* on 20 April 1969, when *Suhaili* was just two days away from Falmouth. The page was dominated by a photograph of Knox-Johnston sitting on *Suhaili*'s coachroof waving to the people aboard the MV *Fathomer*. After the photograph was taken, it was, apparently, transmitted to the mainland by a special radio-telephoto link.

Fathomer was a former Air Sea Rescue boat which had been chartered by the *Sunday Mirror* specifically to greet *Suhaili* as she approached the finish. In fact she – along with the *Queen of the Isles*, an Isles of Scilly passenger vessel on board which were Knox-Johnston's parents – ventured almost 300 miles south-west of Falmouth to do so.

Knox-Johnston first saw these two vessels in the early hours of 19 April.

They closed in with flash bulbs popping and I was able to speak directly to Mother and Father for the first time in 309 days. It was a wonderful moment, but conversation was difficult in the rising wind and sea, and all too soon I had to give up trying to make myself heard and concentrate on reducing sail.

In fact, the worsening conditions soon developed into a storm and Bruce Maxwell, who was aboard the *Fathomer*, later wrote that the waves were so high that *Suhaili* kept disappearing from view. During the storm Knox-Johnston told Maxwell in a radio call that he had hove-to. 'The old girl has taken a bit of a bashing in the last ten months and I don't want to overstrain her,' he said.

On the afternoon of 21 April, a few hours after he sighted Bishop's Rock lighthouse, the welcoming party began to grow:

> A couple of helicopters clattered overhead with cameramen hanging crazily out of open doors, and craft of all shapes and sizes joined us ... A Coastal Command Shackleton appeared on the scene and made half a dozen low level runs over the little convoy, scattering the helicopters out of its path like startled chickens.

It was then that Knox-Johnston first saw the minesweeper HMS *Warsash*, a Royal Naval Reserve ship: 'a wonderful choice of ship in view of my RNR connections, and when I saw her I would not have changed her for a dozen aircraft carriers.' Soon afterwards, he was delighted to see that his three brothers were on board.

The Sunday Times and *Times* newspapers, meanwhile, chartered the motor yacht *Marsupeda* from which, on 21 April, it was reported that *Suhaili* touched eight knots and that Knox-Johnston had said that he would have to take in some sail to allow him to slow down, as he didn't want to arrive in the middle of the night. The report said that Knox-Johnston was looking remarkably fit and that he was prancing around *Suhaili's* sun-bleached deck looking like a holiday maker out for a weekend sailing. His boat wasn't looking so good, however, as she apparently showed the hammering she had taken. Her sails resembled parchment paper, the hull was streaked with rust, and there was not an inch of varnish to be seen.

On the morning of 22 April, *Suhaili* passed the Manacles while, according to Knox-Johnston, 'the convoy was growing hourly'. *Suhaili* was soon joined by the Falmouth lifeboat and the tug *St Mawes* with her funnel repainted in the colours of the British-India Steam Navigation Company. The *Falmouth Packet* later reported:

> Ships, tugs and yachts, dressed overall, hooted, whistled, and boomed their welcome as *Suhaili* glided past in the fitful April sunlight. Overhead, buzzing like tiny motor mowers, were three private helicopters hired by Press and television, and one large chopper belonging to the RN Air Station Culdrose.

While *Suhaili* was battering her way to the finish line – Knox-Johnston later described the last four days as 'the most trying of the voyage, partly because I was so close to home but couldn't get there and partly because nowhere else have I run into weather like I have had' – Falmouth was preparing to welcome him. 'Robin to get the welcome of a lifetime,' read the headline in the *Sunday Mirror* on 13 April, and it would be a welcome home he would never forget. Twelve members of his family were reported to be arriving at a local hotel and they would be accompanied by the press. On 18 April, when it was still optimistically expected that *Suhaili* would finish a couple of days later, the *Falmouth Packet* reported that 'Falmouth once again provides the stage this weekend for another great saga of the sea, when lone sailor Robin Knox-Johnston arrives in the port, the first man to circumnavigate the globe non-stop.'

A few days later, the same newspaper reported on *Suhaili's* triumphant arrival:

> Several thousand people crowded on to Pendennis Point and along Castle Drive ... Before the lone sailor's arrival, traffic, which had been reduced to a crawl by mid-morning, came to a standstill as sightseers abandoned their cars to gain vantage points ... Hundreds took an unofficial day off and visitors came from as far away as Kinlochleven in Scotland and New York. The coastguard was relaying frequent messages regarding Knox-Johnston's predicted arrival time but, when the magic words '*Suhaili* in sight' were chalked up, almost immediately everyone scurried for shelter as the darkest storm clouds and the strongest winds of the day hit Pendennis Point. Knox-Johnston sailed into view only half a mile off St Anthony Head, and a number of small boats emerged from the harbour to swell the flotilla of vessels surrounding him to thirty. Then, as *Suhaili* crossed the finishing line

at Black Rock to the firing of a cannon, the crowd erupted into prolonged cheering. Ships sounded their sirens and motorists their car horns.

In the entrance to the Carrick Roads, the mile-wide stretch of water that divides Falmouth from St Mawes, Black Rock is a drying rock marked by a beacon in an otherwise deep water channel. When *Suhaili* set sail 312 days earlier, she had passed to the east of Black Rock, but on her return she passed to the west, and so crossed a line between the rock and Pendennis Point which has been used to start and finish numerous offshore races since then. As soon as he crossed the line, the first person to board *Suhaili* was a customs officer who asked the traditional question: 'Where from?'

'Falmouth,' replied Knox-Johnston.

Suhaili was then taken in tow by the harbourmaster's launch *Arwenack*, while Knox-Johnston's three brothers climbed aboard and helped to stow the sails and make *Suhaili* shipshape. According to *The West Briton*, Knox-Johnston then 'accepted champagne and drank it straight from the bottle. He quaffed a can of ale and waved as the crowd roared from Castle Drive, from the shipyard jetties and along the waterfront to the yacht club.'

After *Suhaili* was made fast to a mooring, a 'veteran ex-tug skipper' rowed Knox-Johnston ashore in a dinghy to the Royal Cornwall Yacht Club, where he arrived at about 5 p.m., 'looking supremely fit,' according to the *Falmouth Packet*:

[Waiting] to greet him as he took his first faltering steps ashore after the swaying, pitching existence of 10½ months, were the Mayor and Mayoress of Falmouth, the Town Clerk, two civic macebearers, Sir Francis Chichester, and the Missions to Seamen chaplain the Rev David Roberts, who had been one of the last people to bid him farewell when he left Falmouth last June … Incredibly for a man whose canvas-shoed feet had not touched dry land for close on a year, Knox-Johnston wavered and tottered for the first few paces before stepping firmly up the concrete slipway and over the hastily-laid red carpet, escorted by the yacht club Commodore Mr Philip Fox … In a crowd of pallid and chilled faces waiting on the shore he appeared like a bronzed and finely chiselled Adonis, wearing well-polished brown leather shoes, well-pressed grey slacks and a new hand-knitted mustard-coloured Arran sweater. The Mayor shook him firmly by the hand and told him of the hundreds of messages of congratulation which had been arriving at Falmouth all that day.

The Mayor thanked him on behalf of the Queen and the Duke of Edinburgh, and read telegrams of congratulations from the Prime Minister and Edward Heath, the Leader of the Opposition and himself a keen sailor.

A few days later, the front page of the *Falmouth Packet* featured a photograph of Knox-Johnston shaking hands with Sir Francis Chichester, 'the man who charted the course for this young adventurer to follow,' with the headline 'FROM ONE GREAT ENGLISHMAN TO ANOTHER.'

Yachting Monthly also later reported the scene:

> His arrival was, naturally, far from unobtrusive. At the request of the race organisers he was brought ashore at the Royal Cornwall YC slip, where many members of the public had an excellent view but where, had it been necessary, he could have been shielded from over-exposure to the enthusiastic crowds. In the event he was more normal than many of us would have been after 10 days non-stop rather than 10 months.

Having been greeted at the yacht club, Knox-Johnston was taken in an open top car through the streets of Falmouth to the Municipal Buildings for a press conference. Before it could start, however, he had to respond to the crowds of people outside who were chanting 'we want Robin' by putting in the first of two appearances on the balcony. Having been introduced by the Mayor, he thanked the people of Falmouth for the warmth of the reception they had given him and then added that he found it 'a little overwhelming'.

The press conference itself – attended by 'about fifty journalists from the world's Press and TV,' according to the *Falmouth Packet* – was opened by Sir Francis Chichester, who began by announcing that Knox-Johnston had been officially declared the winner of the Golden Globe trophy. Knox-Johnston then expressed his surprise at the extent of the welcome he had received:

> You are attaching a lot of importance to what I consider was a very nice holiday … I didn't fully realise how people were taking this. Personally I felt that I was just taking part in a race and wanting to win it.

He then talked about the particular difficulties of the adverse weather over the previous few days:

Then as I approached Falmouth all those boats came out to meet me, then the yachts came out of the harbour and I thought to myself 'you mustn't let those local yachtsmen show you up' ... I felt I could not disgrace *Suhaili* by heaving-to and waiting for calmer conditions.

Chichester joined Knox-Johnston for his second appearance on the balcony of the Municipal Buildings and took the opportunity to talk to the crowd about the extent of the younger man's accomplishment:

Robin Knox-Johnston is the first man who has been round the world non-stop in anything. Six competitors in the race had to give up for various reasons after they had completed seven or eight thousand miles. Ten years ago even that would have been considered a major achievement.

In the conversation between the two solo circumnavigators published in *The Sunday Times* the following weekend, Chichester expressed admiration for the way in which Knox-Johnston had been able to come ashore in great shape, go through the official reception and then attend a party that lasted until six in the morning.

Four days after arriving in Falmouth, Knox-Johnston and *Suhaili* set sail again, bound for the Thames. This time, however, far from being single-handed, he had a crew of four – his brother Michael, his friend Kenneth Parker and two men from the *Sunday Mirror*. 'Crowds lined the Custom House Quay' to see him off, according to the *Falmouth Packet* and, once again *Suhaili* was accompanied by the *Arwenack*, as far as the harbour entrance. When she reached London, *Suhaili* was lifted out of the water and put on public display in Holborn Circus for two weeks.

'MacArthur, 28, was waved in by Claude Breton, an official of the World Speed Sailing Records Council, sitting aloft a lighthouse on the tiny French island of Ushant,' reported *The Daily Telegraph* on 8 February 2005. This signalled the moment that she crossed the official finish line, between Ushant and the Lizard Point, as did the gun that was fired from the River-class patrol vessel HMS *Severn* nearby. She later wrote that she 'slumped down' on *B&Q*'s cockpit floor, and of her enormous relief that it was over and the record was secured.

Very soon after MacArthur finished, the wind died away and she then savoured the last moments she would have alone aboard *B&Q*. But it wasn't long before she saw members of her shore crew, who had been waiting on board HMS *Severn*, heading towards her in a RIB. She was absolutely thrilled to see them as the clambered aboard *B&Q*. 'I nearly exploded with happiness,' she later wrote.

As soon as her team took control of *B&Q*, MacArthur took to her bunk for her first spell of relaxed sleep for seventy-two days and nights. As she lay there her medic, Dr Kevin McMeel, who had been on call throughout the voyage, took blood samples. Edward Gorman had written in that morning's *Times*:

So concerned are her shore team about her physical and mental state after weeks of sleep deprivation and psychological stress that they are taking no chances with their skipper and she will be immediately assessed by the team doctor as soon as she crosses the finish line.

But it wasn't long before she fell asleep to the unfamiliar sound of people talking and laughing on deck.

She awoke around dawn to see a few accompanying RIBs as well as HMS *Severn*, and was then thrilled to see the gradually expanding flotilla of boats heading out from Falmouth to welcome her home, especially as it was early February.

She soon saw Mark Turner approaching in a RIB and, as he climbed aboard *B&Q*'s stern, they hugged firmly and they both sobbed with pleasure

By now, messages of congratulation were coming in. HM the Queen said:

I am delighted to learn that you have completed your round-the-world journey in record time. I send you my warmest congratulations on your remarkable and historic achievement. Since you set sail last November your progress has been followed by many people in Britain and throughout the world, who have been impressed by your courage, skill and stamina.

The Prince of Wales said:

[We] have all watched your progress with the greatest possible excitement over the past 71 days and our sense of relief at having you home, and pride in your record-breaking achievement, are boundless. The whole of the United Kingdom is delighted by your success – and particularly all those at the Prince's Trust, for whom you are such a wonderful ambassador.

Prime Minister Tony Blair said:

This is a stunning achievement. The whole country is very proud of Ellen.

The *Falmouth Packet* later reported that the first person on land to see *B&Q*, at 8.15 a.m. on 8 February when she was about 16 miles away, was probably the volunteer watchkeeper at Bass Point lookout station on the Lizard peninsula. But there were a great many more people waiting to welcome MacArthur home. 'Falmouth gears up to welcome Ellen,' *The West Briton* headline had read the previous week. 'From Saturday, everyone will be on standby for a huge party and a large daylight screen will be erected in the square, counting down the hours and minutes until Ellen's arrival.' Sure enough, as she approached the finish line, according to *The Daily Telegraph*, 'hundreds gathered in front of a giant screen erected in front of the maritime museum, and cheers and whoops erupted from the crowd as Breton called the giant yacht across the line.'

'Ellen's well-wishers flock to Pendennis Point,' ran the headline in the *Falmouth Packet* later that week. Some, apparently, had come from:

[As] far as Carlisle and Dorset. They were there to give Ellen MacArthur a homecoming to beat all homecomings and one she will certainly not forget in a very long time. Many ... arrived as early as 7am to ensure they got a clear view ... as she arrived back in Falmouth. Those who arrived later had to negotiate the jammed, tree-lined narrow road leading down to the car park at the tip of the point ... The sun broke through the rain clouds as the large flotilla of small boats and craft, including pilot gigs, escorted Ellen past the headland.

As *B&Q* came into the Carrick Roads, a gun was fired from Pendennis Castle to welcome her. ITN's chief newsreader Mark Austin came alongside *B&Q* in a RIB and conducted a live interview with MacArthur while she knelt on the port float. 'I can't begin to comprehend this reception,' she told him.

Knox-Johnston with Falmouth lifeboat coxswain Toby West soon after the end of his voyage. (Image Delivery)

Suhaili approaching the finishing line off Pendennis Point, Falmouth, with a flotilla of well-wishers. (Image Delivery)

Suhaili, with Dodman Point in the background, beating the last few miles towards Falmouth under jib and mizzen. (Image Delivery)

Knox-Johnston in *Suhaili*'s cockpit approaching Falmouth. (Image Delivery)

Suhaili alongside the harbour wall in Flushing not long after the end of the voyage. (Image Delivery)

Knox-Johnston in Falmouth's Chain Locker pub soon after the end of his voyage. (Image Delivery)

Suhaili just off Pendennis Point. (Image Delivery)

B&Q approaching Falmouth at the end of her voyage. (Image Delivery)

B&Q approaching Falmouth at the journey's end (Castorama, like B&Q, is a Kingfisher brand and the names of the two companies were displayed on opposite sides of the mainsail). (Image Delivery)

B&Q moored alongside at Port Pendennis Marina, Falmouth, at the end of her voyage. (Image Delivery)

MacArthur is greeted by friends and family – including her parents, Ken and Avril – at Port Pendennis Marina, Falmouth, at the end of her voyage. (Image Delivery)

Sir Robin Knox-Johnston with Ellen MacArthur at Round Pond, Hyde Park, London, with model yachts. (Credit: Jon Nash/PPL)

'It'sabsolutely incredible. Who would expect anything like this? Unbelievable, So many people, the middle of winter on a weekday. I'm speechless … I feel absolutely elated … over the moon.' The interview over, Austin then turned to camera and said: 'She has now put herself amongst the greatest sailors of all time, perhaps at the top of the list.'

As *B&Q* approached the town of Falmouth itself, the maritime museum came into view and she later wrote that it was 'comforting' to be coming back to a familiar place after such an extreme experience.

MacArthur was 'moved to tears' according to *The Daily Telegraph* when her parents, Ken and Avril, climbed aboard as soon as *B&Q* was moored up at Port Pendennis Marina and 'hugged her, to the delight of the crowds at the Cornish port.'

In front of a huge cheering crowd, MacArthur then lit two hand-held distress flares and, one held aloft in each hand, danced around the trampoline between *B&Q*'s hulls 'like a hyperactive toddler,' according to *The Daily Telegraph*. 'It is amazing what a good night's sleep can do.'

Able Cadet Chris Newcombe from the Falmouth and Penryn Sea Cadet Unit had been chosen to pipe MacArthur ashore, while other sea cadets formed a guard of honour. She then made her way to the stage in Events' Square where, according to the *Falmouth Packet*, 'the atmosphere was thick with anticipation' and where 'the crowd sent up a roar that could have been heard on the Moor' (which is about half a mile away).

There were no formal presentations involving any local dignitaries because, as the organisers of the event later explained, 'Team Ellen simply wanted the welcome to be "by the people and without any formality" and had refused all requests for formal presentations which they believed would not have fitted with the style of their event.'

There was one presentation, however, and that was the Omega Solo Round the World Trophy. Furthermore, just as Sir Francis Chichester had been in Falmouth to welcome Knox-Johnston thirty-six years earlier, Knox-Johnston himself was there to do the same for MacArthur now. Earlier in the day he had gone out to meet *B&Q* in the Falmouth pilot boat and now he was greeting her with a big hug on stage in front of thousands of enthusiastic fans. 'Former record holder greets heroine Ellen,' read the headline in the *Falmouth Packet* a few days later.

Sir Robin was … quick to greet Ellen this week and congratulate her on her achievement. The two found time to talk briefly about their adventures and were clearly happy to be in front of the huge crowds. They may have been far bigger than in 1969 but the welcome was just as warm and sincere then as it was this week.

The Daily Telegraph reported that MacArthur 'addressed the crowd with fluency and self-deprecating wit,' and she told them that 'to see the clock not moving is absolutely unbelievable and I am so relieved.'

She then moved into the maritime museum itself to conduct a press conference in the lecture theatre. She told the enthralled media:

I don't think I can ever manage to communicate how difficult it has been. I know that sounds like a throwaway remark but believe me it was hard. To come here now and look at it all in the past is amazing.

A reporter from the French newspaper *L'Equipe* asked how close she had been to abandoning the attempt at the worst moments. MacArthur – fluent in French – replied:

Près, mais pas prêt. [Close, but not ready.]

MacArthur remained in Falmouth for a few days after she arrived there. Although there were rumours in the local press that she was secretly staying in the Greenbank Hotel, she was actually at the same cottage in which she had waited, over ten weeks earlier, for her weather routers to give her the go-ahead to start her voyage. She then left the town to honour some media commitments in France, but *B&Q* stayed a little longer to allow her engine to be re-installed, and the propeller shaft to be re-fitted by a diver, and eventually left Falmouth on Thursday 17 February.

The local press was justifiably proud of the welcome that the small Cornish town of Falmouth had given both Knox-Johnston and MacArthur. 'Red carpet comes out as town gives Robin a hero's welcome,' read the headline in the *Falmouth Packet* on 25 April 1969. After Knox-Johnston modestly told the enthusiastic crowds that '*Suhaili* would have made it with anybody at the helm. I just went for the holiday,' the same newspaper reported:

> That summed up the character and personality of the 30-year-old Master Mariner of the British India Line who, in a few short hours, endeared himself to the Cornish people who are used to welcoming home heroes of the sea; men like Captain Kurt Carlsen and Mate Dancy of *Flying Enterprise* fame, and lone Atlantic yachtsman Robert Manry.

'Cornwall rolls out the marine equivalent of a red carpet to welcome back Ellen MacArthur more than ten weeks after she left to sail into history,' read *The West Briton* headline on 10 February 2005. 'Ellen's triumph puts town firmly on map' and 'Whole world watches as yachtswoman arrives,' proclaimed the *Falmouth Packet* on the same day. The day after McArthur's arrival a maritime museum official said that 'yesterday meant everything to us … we've shown that Falmouth has the facilities to manage global events' and that 'Falmouth hasn't seen sailing history like this since Robin Knox-Johnston returned to Falmouth.'

The local traders didn't do too badly either. 'The ice cream hut at [Pendennis] Point did a roaring trade,' reported the *Falmouth Packet* in April 1969, 'but many disappointed spectators put their sixpences into the telescope only to find it was out of order for the big event!' While in February 2005, Andrew Baker wrote in *The Daily Telegraph* that 'traffic wardens earned a year's bonus in a couple of hours and the Oggy Oggy pasty shop owner will be contemplating an early and comfortable retirement.'

Tributes

Hardly surprisingly, newspapers and magazines were filled with praise for Knox-Johnston's and MacArthur's astonishing achievements. Even when he was just over halfway around the world *The Sunday Times* thought that Knox-Johnston had 'already shown himself in the class of the seagoing knights, Rose and Chichester' and when he had completed his voyage, his own sponsor the *Sunday Mirror* said that he had sailed 'into immortality'.

The Sunday Times reported two days before Knox-Johnston arrived in Falmouth:

> Somehow we always expect the heroes of outstanding tests of courage and endurance to be cast in a superhuman mould, to have some obvious signs of great distinction about them. Instead we are going to meet a modest young man casual and unassuming about his great feat, rather embarrassed by all the fuss.

'All Hail *Suhaili*' read the headline of an article by the highly-respected sailing writer Jack Knights in *Yachts and Yachting*. Describing the circumnavigation as 'the four-minute mile in the history of the sea', he then wrote that:

> [There] will be faster non-stop roundings, you may be sure, both solo and crewed, but this will always be the very first in the history of mankind and for that reason alone his name will always be remembered.

'Wonderful! Fantastic! A terrific feat of endurance and seamanship,' wrote H. Kahn in *Yachting Monthly* referring to the 'praise uttered by hundreds … We echo this praise to a superb yachtsman whose exploits will go down in the annals of yachting history as one of the greatest of them all.' Kahn went on to say that:

> [What] is very apparent was his stubborn nature and strong determination to finish what he'd set out to do. This spurred him on when most would've thrown in the towel. Coupled with this, and most important of all, was his superb seamanship and wide knowledge and experience of the sea and all its moods.

•◆•

The Times correspondent Simon Barnes compared MacArthur's new record with long standing records in other sports: Jim Laker's 19 wickets in a 1956 test match and Florence Griffith Joyner's 1988 100m and 200m records, all of which still stand today; Bob Beaman's 1968 long jump record which stood for twenty-three years; and Michael Johnson's 1996 200m record, which still stood at the time Barnes wrote his piece but was subsequently broken by Usain Bolt in 2008. 'Ellen MacArthur's feat will place her among the pantheon of sporting greats whose achievements may never be matched,' wrote Barnes who then went on to compare her achievement with those of the Brazilian footballer Pele, the British rower Steve Redgrave and – somewhat misguidedly as it turned out – the now-disgraced American drug cheat cyclist Lance Armstrong.

The Daily Telegraph writer Sue Mott asked if MacArthur was 'the greatest British sailor of all time':

Most right-thinking historians would agree that Nelson was a thoroughgoing hero, and Ellen isn't quite up there yet … So, whether MacArthur is first or tenth in the sailor table doesn't really matter. She has intensified her life and ours. We can only stand on dry land and admire.

Yachts and Yachting's highly respected sailing journalist Bob Fisher wrote:

This achievement ranks high among those obtained by a succession of British mariners dating back as far as Sir Francis Drake … to Sir Francis Chichester. Alongside them are the Admirals, like Lord Nelson, who won major battles at sea and the Olympic Champions like Rodney Pattison, Shirley Robertson and Ben Ainslie, who have all contributed two gold medals to the country's haul in a sport in which the British excel. Dame Ellen MacArthur's achievement is right up there with the very best.

Yachting World's editor Andrew Bray responded to comments, largely in the non-nautical press, that MacArthur couldn't have done what she did without the technology at her disposal and the help of her shore team:

What complete and utter nonsense! Does the fact that Michael Schumacher has a better car and superior race tracks make him less of a driver than Stirling Moss? Or Kelly Holmes having better running shoes make her inferior to Roger Banister? Of course it doesn't. Most experienced and fit yachtsmen would be hard-pushed to sail *B&Q* solo for 24 hours at record pace, however much outside assistance they had, let alone keep that pace right round the world.

Meanwhile, Edward Gorman, the sailing correspondent of *The Times* wrote:

I could never put Ellen or anyone else above Knox-Johnston for what he did in his time, Francis Chichester for what he did, or Chay Blyth – the technology and the world has moved on, so it's very difficult to compare. But I certainly think she merits to be mentioned it the same paragraph as these people.

12

Navigation

In the same way that technological advances during the period between Knox-Johnston's and MacArthur's voyages produced great strides in the world of communications, so it did with navigation and weather forecasting. In 1978, the US government launched the first of a series of satellites which would become the Global Positioning System (GPS). Initially the system was intended for the sole use of the US military but in 1983 – after a Korean passenger plane was shot down when it accidentally strayed into USSR air space – the US government made it available for civilian use. By 1993, the last of the twenty-four satellites necessary for a truly global system was launched. To ascertain a latitude and longitude position, it is necessary for a GPS device to receive signals from three satellites simultaneously and it was now possible to do so anywhere on earth at any time. In 2000, the intentional downgrading of accuracy for civilian users was ended and the system immediately became considerably more accurate. It was now possible to determine a position to within a few metres.

So that was the technology available to MacArthur in 2004, but things were very different for Knox-Johnston thirty-six years earlier. At that time, the only way to navigate when out of sight of land was by sextant, an instrument that had provided the main means of navigation for over 200 years and which had been derived from similar instruments which came before that. The technique involves taking a sight to measure the angle of the sun or other heavenly bodies above the horizon. By subsequent mathematical calculations and reference to sight reduction tables, a position line can then be calculated. If it is possible to take sights of two celestial bodies at the same time, then two position lines will be ascertained and the point at which they intersect will give the position. Latitude can easily be calculated by measuring the altitude of the sun at local noon, simply by observing its climb until it reaches its maximum altitude. This is the one bit of astronavigation for which an accurate chronometer isn't required but, by having one, longitude can also be calculated from a noon sight by checking the time at that moment at the Greenwich meridian. Having established a position by astronavigation, it is possible to continue to navigate until the next opportunity for a sextant sight by monitoring the compass (which gives the direction in which the boat is pointing) and the log (which gives the distance sailed through the water) while also taking into account currents and leeway: a process known as Dead Reckoning. There are many people who fear that today's availability of electronic navigation aids is leading to the demise of astronavigation techniques, but it is perhaps highly significant that the US Navy, which began to phase out astronavigation training for its officers in 2000, reintroduced it in 2016.

Knox-Johnston had a thorough grounding in astronavigation during his apprenticeship with British India, and subsequently had plenty of opportunity to put it into practice during his service with the company, as well as in the RNR and on *Suhaili*'s voyage from India to England. For his circumnavigation, he took with him his 'ageing Plath sextant and an old but reliable chronometer' (the latter is now in the Rolex Museum in Switzerland), a compass and a trailing log. He would have liked to have taken an echo sounder and radio direction finder, both of which would have been particularly useful during the coastal parts of his voyage, but he couldn't afford them. He typically took one sun sight early in the morning for longitude, one at noon for latitude, and if he was approaching land he would take another in the afternoon. But he had problems with all his instruments. On his sixty-sixth day at sea, a wave soaked his sextant just as he was taking a sight. He thought it was undamaged but was concerned that he couldn't dry it properly. Over the following days it received 'repeated soakings' and on one occasion when he lost his balance while using it, he fell to the deck and tried to protect the sextant from damage. He received a bruised arm in the process and subsequently thought that the sextant had a 'considerable error'. But when he checked it again on the next fine day, by taking sights every half hour, he found that it was still accurate. He regularly washed it when it was raining and, although the mirrors tarnished slightly, it continued to work accurately throughout his voyage.

He couldn't always use it, however, as he needed clear skies – at least in way of the sun – to do so. '2 months at sea and I don't know where we are,' he wrote in his logbook on his sixty-first day at sea, after he had been unable to get a longitude fix since earlier that morning and hadn't established his position since some time before that. Furthermore, he thought that a Dead Reckoning position would be just a 'guess' as *Suhaili* had, he thought, steered an erratic course throughout the previous night.

Knox-Johnston reckoned that his chronometer lost, on average, eight and a half seconds a day, a huge amount in terms of accurate astronavigation. Whenever he could, he listened for time checks on his radio receiver but he had one four-week period, while crossing the Pacific, without any such checks, 'which caused [him] considerable worry'. But when he eventually received a BBC time check as he was approaching South America, he found his chronometer was only 3 seconds different from what he expected it to be.

During the first half of his voyage the compass light packed up, and, after about seven months, his last torch gave up, and so, from then on, he identified stars, whenever he could, to set a course at night. He hardly used his trailing log as he thought it was inaccurate, and after a while it became too much of a drag when barnacles grew upon it.

Although his basic but essential instruments worked reliably, Knox-Johnson's worries about them led to specific concerns about his position. On one occasion – when he thought he was 60 miles from the Australian coast – he thought he could detect the 'unmistakeable aroma of land' and there were also large numbers of insect and butterflies in the air around him. He soon realised that the smell was that of the weed around *Suhaili*'s hull which had been dried out by the warm weather he had recently encountered. But he was still concerned about the insects and butterflies, and it was only after he had carefully taken a number of additional sights that his mind was put at rest. 'I came to the conclusion that the butterfly was wrong, not me,' he later wrote.

Amazingly, he used just thirteen charts during his entire circumnavigation, ranging from a detailed one of Falmouth to another called simply '3934 The World'.

Weather and Forecasting

Throughout her record-breaking circumnavigation, MacArthur employed the services of weather routers Commanders' Weather Corporation. At that time, Commanders' Weather employed nine meteorologists with a combined experience of 177 years in weather forecasting, and had around 3,000 clients ranging from round-the-cans racers to superyachts. MacArthur was sometimes in touch with Commanders' Weather up to eight times a day (she always called them rather than the other way around) and she also occasionally used Meeno Schrader, who had been her weather router in the Route du Rhum, as well as frequently discussing weather issues with Mark Turner. She also regularly downloaded GRIB (GRIdded Binary) files – a concise data format commonly used in meteorology to store historical and forecasted weather data. All of that, in theory, provided MacArthur with a wealth of information about the likely weather several days ahead, and allowed her to make tactical decisions to ensure she was able to maximise her time in winds which were favourable in both strength and direction. In conversation with *Yachting World*'s Elaine Bunting before she set off on her circumnavigation, she said:

> Being allowed weather routing makes a big difference. Also just to be able to talk to someone about it … you can discuss it and that helps you learn a lot as well, about the wave patterns or whatever.

Knox-Johnston's weather forecasting equipment was altogether more basic. He carried with him a number of books including *Ocean Passages of the World*, which showed the best routes to follow between ports in different seasons; *Meteorology for Mariners* and various pilot books. The pilot charts he had were divided up into areas which were 5 degrees of latitude by 5 degrees of longitude (which is 300 miles by 300 miles at the equator, but further north and south the longitude distances diminish) and in each of these squares is information on wind (average strength and direction) and other information, such as likelihood of icebergs and tropical storms for each month of the year. All of that information is based on countless observations that have been made over many years but it is, of course, a statistical average and the actual weather can be very different.

The nearest thing he had to any sort of electronic instrument was a barometer – which, incidentally, he borrowed from a public house in Falmouth shortly before he departed, and which had the slogan 'Guinness is good for you' inscribed on it – which measures atmospheric pressure: a fall in pressure can be a useful warning of bad weather approaching. On his 216th day at sea, for instance, when he was about 200 miles from Cape Horn he wrote in his logbook:

> The glass is depressed. It's dropped over a millibar an hour since 0500 and I am worried. It's never dropped quite like this before and we are in an area famous for its rough seas … I don't mind admitting I feel a bit scared tonight.

He had good reason to be scared – that night it blew Force 10. Occasionally, when he was in range, he also benefited from weather forecasts broadcast by radio, but otherwise he was entirely dependent on his own visual observations. These, however, only gave him warnings of imminent weather changes: low black clouds warning of squalls, for instance, or falling seawater temperatures indicating that there might be icebergs in the area.

There were times when he was puzzled by the weather he was experiencing, and came to reasoned, but inconclusive, suppositions. He wrote in his log on his 180th day at sea, as he was crossing the Pacific Ocean, that:

'... [We're] bashing into fresh to strong SE winds. But the really puzzling thing is the sea. After these days of steady SE winds they should be from the same direction, but they're not. As far as I can tell we have waves from the east, south-east and south, and swell from the east and south-east. This rather points to a recent change in wind direction and in that case we may be in the middle or near the front of an easterly air stream that is moving east at about the same speed as ourselves.

MacArthur generally had a considerably better idea of the configuration of the weather systems around her, and of their likely development. Sometimes, however, this simply gave her advance warning of fearful conditions that she couldn't avoid. For instance, on her twenty-second day at sea, when she was south-east of the Cape of Good Hope, she was particularly concerned about a big depression which, even though it was six days away, she didn't think she would be able to avoid. Over the next few days, she monitored the situation closely. On day twenty-four it looked as if it would bring consistent 50-knot winds and she was wondering if she might be able to head north to avoid it; the next day she realised that going north wouldn't allow her to escape it, and she thought that it would bring 'survival conditions' for a while; on day twenty-six she knew that she was facing several days of particularly bad weather; and two days later – 25 December – she wrote that 'the only thing white about this Christmas is the breaking waves all around us.' (In an unintentional but neat parallel with Knox-Johnston's thoughts on the Apollo 8 mission around the moon thirty-six years earlier, MacArthur later commented that the nearest human beings to her at that time were the astronauts on the International Space Station.) Just two days later, she knew she was in a much better situation when *B&Q* was sailing at the same speed as an east-moving front.

However, despite the great support and array of technology at her disposal, there were times when the information she received wasn't as accurate as she would have hoped. On her thirty-first day at sea, she had 36 knots of wind and Commanders' Weather were predicting that it would increase. So she was reefed appropriately but the wind actually dropped to 25 knots. She eventually increased sail after *B&Q* spent five hours sailing a couple of knots slower than she could have been. She berated herself for not following her own instincts because her own observations – clearing blue sky and increasing sea temperature – had been indicating that the wind would drop. And on day sixty-seven she wrote about the 'unreliability of the weather models and forecasts'.

•◆•

Strong winds and the accompanying big seas are always a huge threat for ocean sailors, particularly those sailing single-handed, and both of our circumnavigators had their fair share. *Suhaili's* knock-down when she was 700 miles south-west of the Cape of Good Hope caused a great deal of damage, and also had a profound effect on Knox-Johnston. He told the *Sunday Mirror* – whose front-page headline read 'I've Capsized – Dramatic Call From The Lone Sailor' – that it was the worst storm he had ever experienced, and that he thought it was the end. On the same day *The Sunday Times* headline said 'Giant Wave Hits Leader'. But not long afterwards he experienced five gales in ten days, which prompted him to later write: 'the frequency of the gales appalled me'. On his 121st day at sea, he experienced a Force 10 which he described 'the worst weather I have ever encountered'. He couldn't see how *Suhaili* could survive such conditions and he seriously considered taking to his life raft – about two thousand miles from Australia – before realising that he was far better off remaining on board his boat while she was still afloat. 'Day succeeds weary day and gale succeeds gale,' he later reported. 'I'm getting thoroughly sick of it all. There's no respite.'

But the time he was in the greatest danger was on his way to his New Zealand rendezvous with Bruce Maxwell. Initially he thought he would be meeting off Bluff, which is on the north side of the Foveaux Strait. Before making his approach, he heard a New Zealand radio weather forecast, which said that a depression was on its way across the Tasman Sea, but he expected it to pass to the south of his position. However, when he was about to enter the Foveaux Strait and it was too late to change his plan, he became aware (from the falling barometer and a further forecast) that Force 9 to 10 winds were heading his way. Sure enough, during the course of that night he found himself sailing, under storm jib alone, in very strong winds and in appalling visibility. He trailed a sea anchor and a 720ft-long warp to slow *Suhaili* as he was not entirely sure of his exact position. The following morning he saw land to leeward and realised he would have to alter course to try to claw his way away from it. He realised that he would not manage to do so under storm jib alone so he decided to set more sail, even though he was seriously worried that the rig would not be able to take the strain. 'Better to run ashore without sails or mast than do nothing to try to get her off,' he later wrote. The trailing warp and sea anchor were now a hindrance but it took a superhuman effort to bring them back aboard as they were 'hopelessly entangled'. Eventually he realised that he and *Suhaili* had won this particular battle and they were clear of the lee shore. It subsequently took him three days to untangle the warp and sea anchor.

MacArthur never had a lee shore to worry about, but the effect of ocean waves on *B&Q* frequently gave her cause for concern. On her fourteenth day at sea, she wrote:

> The waves are absolutely huge and in this breeze we are just flying off them and coming crashing down. The noise the boat is making is horrendous – as are the noises I am making as I'm bouncing off the sides of the boat. I've been thrown off the chart table seat, I've had my head thrown against the roof of the boat and my feet thrown against the floor on numerous occasions.

More often than not, especially during dark nights, it was the anticipation of how *B&Q* might land at the bottom of a wave that worried her.

On her twenty-ninth day at sea she wrote that she had had 'a day from hell with horrendous conditions'. *B&Q* had been picked up by a freak wave which frightened MacArthur more than at any previous time and another wave broke over the boat 'as if an elephant had been dropped from heaven'.

But, as she rounded the Horn in winds gusting over 50 knots and with just the storm jib up – it was the first time the mainsail had been down since she left Falmouth and *B&Q* was still surfing at 30 knots – she wrote that she couldn't help feeling that she would 'miss this wild and wonderful place'.

However, while strong winds and big seas caused concern for both circumnavigators, light winds, variable winds and winds in an unfavourable direction caused them great frustration. Both of them were, after all, trying to get around the world as quickly as possible.

Knox-Johnston's greatest frustration was the long periods of easterly winds he experienced in an area where it was perfectly reasonable for him to expect favourable westerlies. When he left New Zealand, he decided to keep north of the 44-degrees South line of latitude – until such time as he would have to dip south to round Cape Horn – to minimise the chances of encountering icebergs. Over the following three weeks, the wind blew from a generally easterly direction on all but one day. On his 179th day at sea, he wrote in his log that *Suhaili* was 'north of the 40th parallel and at present steering for Alaska! … I doubt if I'll remain sane for much longer.' Three days later, when he was as far north as the 37th parallel, he decided to head south again, or even west of south, until he found the westerlies he needed, even if that meant straying into iceberg territory. As it happens, he encountered westerlies after three days, but by this time he thought he had lost about ten days and that this might mean the difference between winning and losing the Golden Globe. But, a fortnight later, when *Suhaili* was 1700 miles from Cape Horn, he encountered easterlies again. 'I just give up!' he wrote in his log. 'Someone is going to have to rewrite the books or there has been a general and consistent misprint!' Eventually, on 1 January, seventeen days before he rounded the Horn, he began to get winds from a more favourable direction.

For MacArthur, the fact that her trimaran was hugely vulnerable to being caught out with too much sail up in sudden squalls, and that she was, at every minute of every day, completely aware of how she was faring against the record, the need to do everything she could to ensure she had the right amount of sail up at all times, and to be heading in the best direction, was particularly acute. Furthermore, simply because of the size of her boat, the effort she needed to put into tacking, gybing and changing sails was especially great – and put that effort in she did. Throughout her voyage, she frequently wrote of the scale of the tasks, and towards the end she knew that sail changes were taking twice as long as at the beginning because she was so tired. On day twenty-nine, for instance, she made twelve sail changes in eight hours, going from triple-reefed mainsail and staysail to full main and genoa. Eight days later, a wind varying from 5 to 38 knots and changing in direction by 60 degrees at times, forced eleven sail changes in twenty-four hours, and she later wrote that she had never previously experienced such unpredictable conditions. She wrote further, on day forty-four, about the difficulty of selecting the right sails in squally weather when she knew she had too little sail up to make good progress, and of her exhaustion after the number of sail changes she had made in the previous twenty-four hours.

Three days later, she found herself with a triple-reefed mainsail in winds of just 3 knots when she had been expecting 40 knots, all too aware of the consequences of increasing sail if the forecast wind did then arrive. Again, she wrote of her exhaustion having made twelve sail changes in twelve hours.

On her sixty-eighth day at sea, with the wind varying between 4 and 22 knots and going round in circles, she gybed seven times in two hours, and on her last night at sea with wind up to 40 knots and shifting through 100 degrees, she tacked eleven times.

For any boat, the consequences of hitting an iceberg in the Southern Ocean would be catastrophic. For the most part, Knox-Johnston sailed north of the expected ice limit – although, when he decided to go south in search of westerly winds after three weeks of predominantly easterlies, he found that his Admiralty Pilot and his chart gave conflicting information regarding the limit: the chart showed it further south and, as it had been published more recently, he chose to put his faith in that, a decision that he later described as 'unwise'.

B&Q's course across the Southern Ocean was, for the most part, further south than *Suhaili*'s. Although the trimaran was fitted with radar which might give a better warning of an iceberg than MacArthur's visual lookout in poor visibility or at night, or when she was down below, it is likely that the boat's high speed would mean there would be very little time to take evasive action.

As she was approaching the Kerguelen islands, she was aware that there had been reports of icebergs closer to New Zealand than there would normally be and she thought that she would have to go south of them, which she thought would be 'pretty stressful'. Sure enough, soon after she passed south of New Zealand, she saw two icebergs to the north of her position. Although she found it hard to gauge how big they were, she thought that one of them might have been the size of a large container ship. A few days later, when she had heard a report that Nick Maloney (competing in the Vendée Globe) had seen icebergs the previous day in the same area where she was now, she again saw two to the north. She was particularly surprised and concerned about this, because normally they would have been 300 miles to the south.

After the conclusion of his voyage, Knox-Johnston analysed what he might have done better to make the best of the weather conditions to achieve a faster circumnavigation. He realised that he probably lost a week or two on his outward passage in the South Atlantic by heading for the Cape of Good Hope too early rather than heading south until he found himself in strong westerly winds; he lost more time by sailing into the Australian Bight in order to try to sight a ship; and, of course, after he encountered easterlies soon after he left New Zealand, he should have headed south in search of westerlies sooner. In all, he considered that these 'errors' cost him between three weeks and a month.

Repairs and Maintenance

However well-built and prepared a boat is, long voyages and extreme weather take their toll, and it is a vitally important characteristic of solo sailors that they must be able to make any necessary repairs quickly and effectively if they are to have any chance of achieving their goals. Both Knox-Johnston and MacArthur were clearly particularly skilful in this respect, and even gained a certain amount of enjoyment and satisfaction from the tasks they had to undertake.

Knox-Johnston became aware of a potentially serious problem that could easily force him to give up just a fortnight into his voyage. 'She is taking in more water than she should,' he wrote in his logbook on day sixteen. He was having to pump the bilges at least twice a day, and he suspected that *Suhaili* was leaking through the seams along the garboards, the planks nearest the wood keel. He knew that he would have to fix this problem if he was going to be able to continue. He bided his time until he found himself in relatively calm and warm waters just south of the Cape Verde islands. Wearing a mask and snorkel, he dived over the side and was almost immediately able to see the problem: on both sides of the boat there was a noticeable gap in the seams over a length of about eight feet, and he could even see this gap opening and closing as *Suhaili* moved gently in the slight swell. He climbed back on board, smoked a cigarette and considered his options. He decided that the only real solution was to caulk the seams, but how he was going to do so was another matter: this was, after all, a job which in normal circumstances would be done with the boat dried out.

He began by preparing some caulking cotton by twisting it and cutting it into 18-inch (0.45m) lengths. He was all too aware that caulking should be done with much longer lengths but realised that wouldn't be possible under water. He was concerned that there might be sharks in the area so, wearing a blue shirt and jeans which he hoped would be less visible than his relatively white body, he dived over the side again. He tried hammering the cotton into the seams – initially with his largest screwdriver and then with a proper caulking iron – but found it an impossible task as he was unable to hold his breath for long enough to make any progress. Each time he came up for air and then dived back down, he found that the cotton he had just forced into the seam had come out again.

He climbed back on board to think again. He then sewed the twisted cotton onto a 1½in (38mm) width of canvas long enough to repair the whole seam, and then coated it with Stockholm tar. Back under the water, he forced the cotton into the seams and fixed the canvas to the adjacent timber with copper tacks. He was concerned that this might get ripped off by *Suhaili*'s ongoing motion so he went back on board and began to prepare some copper strip (which had been left on board by the Marconi radio engineers) to tack over the top of the canvas. It was then that he realised that his earlier fears that he might not be alone were not unfounded. A single shark circled *Suhaili* for about ten minutes before Knox-Johnston, fearing that it might never go away, shot it. He then waited for half an hour in case other sharks came to investigate before diving below again and completing the repair on the port side. He had been in the water for about four hours and was not altogether sorry when a light wind prevented him from continuing. He completed the repairs to the starboard side two days later and for the rest of the voyage the leaks in *Suhaili*'s hull were considerably reduced.

Suhaili's knock-down – on her eighty-sixth day at sea when she was about 700 miles south-west of the Cape of Good Hope – had serious repercussions for the structure of the coachroof, the self-steering gear, the radio and the water supply.

While he was clearing up the appalling mess inside the cabin after the capsize, Knox-Johnston noticed 'ominous cracks' around the edge of the coachroof and he was faced with the very real possibility that the whole structure could be swept away by a big wave. This would leave him sailing an open boat in the Southern Ocean, the thought of which gave him 'a sick feeling in the pit of my stomach', hardly surprising as his chances of survival would have been negligible. However, after he spent all of the following day reinforcing the structure with the biggest bolts and screws that he had on board, he was confident that it would remain intact, although it continued to leak in various places throughout the voyage.

It was the water damage from this same incident which, from then on, gave him problems with his long-range radio transmitter. He had several attempts to repair it, including two whole days when he was approaching Australia, but all to no avail. 'I might as well have tried to sort out a railway timetable,' he later wrote.

When Knox-Johnston left Falmouth, he had 15 gallons of fresh water in polythene containers in addition to the water he had in *Suhaili's* main water tanks. By the time of the knockdown he hadn't touched the water in the main tanks and still had 10 gallons in the containers as he had managed to keep them reasonably topped up by catching rain water in the Doldrums. But sometime afterwards, he discovered that the water in the tanks had become contaminated and was now a 'pale brown and rather unpleasant smelling liquid'. He was about 400 miles south of Cape Town at that time and considered heading there, but then decided that the usable fresh water he had would last forty days and in that time he would almost reach Australia, and that there would be a good chance of collecting more rainwater along the way. 'Showers help Robin,' read the headline in the *Sunday Mirror* on 22 September, showing how quickly he was able to develop an efficient system for collecting water in heavy rainfall. Throughout the rest of his voyage he continued to collect water at every opportunity. On his 254th day at sea, for instance, he collected a total of nine gallons from the mizzen in as many hours. 'It was pouring off so fast that I held the container under the gooseneck and did not bother with the bucket,' he wrote in his log.

As part of Knox-Johnston's preparations for his circumnavigation, he needed to fit a self-steering system. He had a particular problem to overcome,

149

however, in that *Suhaili's* mizzen boom extended 6 feet (1.8m) beyond her stern and would have quickly destroyed the upper part of a conventional wind-vane system. Knox-Johnston's ingenious solution was to fit two wind vanes, each mounted on a stainless-steel structure protruding from the sides of the boat and level with the mizzen mast. These would be connected by a system of ropes and pulleys to the auxiliary rudder. *Yachting World* later described it as a 'somewhat Heath Robinson looking and complicated twin-vane assembly' and *The Sunday Times* thought it gave *Suhaili* a 'wallowing trawler appearance'. Knox-Johnston himself thought it 'looked about as decorative as a piece of scaffolding' but came to refer to it affectionately as The Admiral.

In the early part of the voyage, the system didn't work particularly well in light winds but Knox-Johnston managed to solve this by modifying some nylon bushes which had been seizing up and causing friction. During the knockdown, the port wind vane and its stanchion were seriously damaged, but Knox-Johnston was able to make a satisfactory repair a couple of days later, although he was completely immersed in the sea while doing so as *Suhaili* was rolling heavily at the time. Just three days after that, the self-steering rudder broke. He had a spare which he was able to fit – although, once again, he got completely soaked as he had to get into the water to do it – but he became particularly concerned that this breakage should happen so early in the voyage and that he no longer had a spare. So he then spent three days making a new blade from a teak bunk board and modifying its installation in a way that he hoped would be stronger.

Six weeks later, when *Suhaili* was in the Australian Bight, this rudder broke. Knox-Johnston replaced it with the original, now repaired, blade. He knew it wouldn't last but 'the thought was a bit depressing so I thought about other things.'

During the latter part of the Pacific crossing, some time after the self-steering system had finally packed up and Knox-Johnston had learned to manage without it, he became concerned that the increasingly damaged self-steering structure would become a hazard and so, about 1,000 miles from Cape Horn, he cut it away. 'Suddenly *Suhaili* was smaller,' he wrote, 'but she seemed more comfortable in herself, rather like an old lady who has taken off too tight a corset.'

Suhaili suffered various damage to her rig during the course of her voyage. On both her 114th and 215th days at sea her gooseneck broke, in different places each time. 'This may be the end of it all,' Knox-Johnston wrote in his log on the first occasion. But each time his ingenuity won the day and he was able to sail on.

He had to climb the mast on several occasions: in the Bass Straits to retrieve some broken luff slides, for instance; off Otago after the main halyard had jumped off its sheave and jammed; to reeve a new spinnaker halyard to replace a broken one; and to measure and then fit a new jib stay after some of the strands of the original one broke. The latter job also required him to crawl along the bowsprit while *Suhaili* was pitching so much that the end of the bowsprit was going under water and then up in the air about 15ft. To do the job Knox-Johnston needed a spanner in each hand and he later wrote that he was 'hanging on with my eyelashes'.

The sails needed a great deal of maintenance throughout the voyage, and on the 211th day the mainsail split into two pieces. Knox-Johnston had an old one on board – 'in rather better condition than I thought' – which he was able to use while he carried out lengthy repairs. 'After steering,' he wrote during the latter part of the voyage, 'sewing had become my major occupation.'

On the 100th day of his voyage, Knox-Johnston decided to turn the engine as he hadn't done so for two months, but he found it had seized up. A few days later he had another go at it and managed to start it after removing the electric starter motor and applying significant pressure directly to the flywheel. After persevering for some time, he managed to get it going, but later in the voyage the problem reoccurred. This time he spent two whole days working on it and then returned to it a couple of days later 'determined not to be defeated by an inanimate and uncooperative lump of metal'. On this occasion, however, he was defeated but hardly surprisingly, because after the voyage ended it was found that the engine had two cracked cylinders and needed to be completely replaced.

At times during the course of his circumnavigation, Knox-Johnston felt overwhelmed by *Suhaili*'s repair issues and considered retiring. The first time was on day fifty-three, when he was first concerned that the gooseneck might break, the brake on the main halyard winch had failed and the cabin top was suffering from leaks. 'None of them is disastrous taken by itself but the combination could be,' he wrote in his log.

He next considered retiring to Melbourne when the self-steering finally packed up. 'Here I was not even halfway round the world and with no self-steering. I could draw little encouragement to continue the voyage without it from the state of the boat.' He then considered the problems he had with the tiller, the rudder bearings, radio transmitter, the engine, and various leaks:

> These were the physical reasons for heading for Melbourne and giving up, and the more I considered it then the more I felt that it would be foolish to go on, particularly as I still had Cape Horn ahead of me … And yet I was in the lead … and I was way ahead of my nearest competitor … *Suhaili* was the smallest boat ever to make the voyage to Australia non-stop, but wouldn't it be a much finer thing to be the first man round the world non-stop? After all I was nearly halfway. It would be a pity to waste all the work so far.

So he decided to carry on, at least as far as New Zealand.

'My Boat is Falling to Pieces,' ran the headline in the *Sunday Mirror* on 24 November, just after Bruce Maxwell had met up with Knox-Johnson off Otago. 'All in all, not a very good picture,' Knox-Johnston told Maxwell after listing *Suhaili*'s various issues. 'However, the hull appears sound and the boat still sails and the quickest way home is to keep going.'

'If the reports of his damaged gear are correct,' Francis Chichester said during his Royal Institution Discourse on 31 January, 'it will be little short of a miracle if he can make it back to Falmouth without putting in somewhere for repairs.' As it happens, not long before that, and just after rounding Cape Horn, Knox-Johnston had taken stock of the situation. 'With 9,000 miles to go *Suhaili* was in reasonable shape,' he wrote, 'and there was no reason why we should not make Falmouth' although 'superficially she looked a mess.'

After *Suhaili* safely returned to Falmouth, Chichester was full of praise for Knox-Johnston's ability to keep his boat going. 'The point is,' he said, 'how many offshore sailors can do repairs like this? Not many I should think.'

B&Q's self-steering gear was an electronic autopilot – in fact she had two, from different manufacturers – which never caused any problems for MacArthur throughout her circumnavigation. However, she needed to produce the electricity to run the pilot, along with many other essential pieces of equipment, and so *B&Q* had two generators. The main one was water-cooled and had an output of 200 amps, and the secondary, back-up, one was air-cooled and could produce 55 amps. Just as Knox-Johnston did, MacArthur made a discovery a couple of weeks into her voyage that might have brought it to a premature end. She found that the water-cooled generator was using far more oil than expected and, at that rate, she would run out of it long before she completed her circumnavigation. So she started using the back-up generator, but its fuel consumption would be greater than the main one so, if she continued to use it, she would run out of diesel. Furthermore this generator produced unbearable fumes inside the cabin (where the temperature went up to 48 degrees with all the hatches open the first time she ran it) although this problem was minimised when MacArthur re-routed the ducting.

Meanwhile, her shore team acquired an identical water-cooled generator and began some experiments into alternative oils which they knew MacArthur had on board. They soon found that the generator would run on a mixture of olive oil and rape seed oil, and they calculated that there was enough of this (and the oil that the generator was supposed to use) on board to run it for about half the voyage, and there would be just enough diesel to run the air-cooled generator for the other half. She needed to run the air-cooled generator for about three hours in every nine, but in certain sea conditions the diesel supply proved unreliable and resulted in an airlock and the need to restart the set with alarming frequency. It was not uncommon for her to have to restart it a dozen times during each charging period and on one occasion six times in twenty-five minutes.

To save weight *B&Q* carried very little fresh water and so MacArthur was almost entirely reliant on her two reverse-osmosis water makers. However, the pipe system for sucking sea water for conversion to fresh water was integrated with the water cooling system for the main generator – so when that wasn't working, there was no replenishment of the fresh water supply. To solve this problem, MacArthur had to squeeze into *B&Q*'s emergency ballast area under the cabin sole – a particularly hazardous place to be as she would be unable to escape in a hurry if she needed to tend to the autopilot or the sheets – where she carried out an ingenious plumbing modification which solved the problem.

In the South Atlantic on the way home, the Solent jib tack line parted. As a result of this, the lower end of its stay broke free, leaving the sail and its furling system blowing free and swinging from its attachment point up the mast. She had to bear away downwind and then winch in on the furling line to bring it back down to the deck. Amazingly the sail was undamaged – in fact *B&Q* suffered from no damage at all to her halyards or sails throughout the voyage – but the furling drum casing fell apart.

Soon after that, *B&Q* suffered her potentially most serious rig problem, when the mainsail headboard car and track were damaged. MacArthur dropped the sail – for only the second time since she left Falmouth – and replaced some missing rods which would act as bearings in the headboard car, and then hoisted it with two reefs. The repairs to the track might well have been a straightforward job on a bench in a workshop, but the positions of the damage, well up the mast at the first and second reef points, and with all movement of the boat greatly exaggerated at those heights, required MacArthur to make a Herculean effort to make the necessary repairs.

For any ocean-going sailing boat, there are concerns about hitting something in the water, but for *B&Q*, at the speeds at which she was frequently travelling, the risk of damage from such a collision was significant. On day twenty-six, the centreboard hit an unidentified object and *B&Q* slowed suddenly from 26 to 14 knots, whereupon MacArthur was thrown forward onto the chart table. Luckily there was no apparent damage – MacArthur thought that the rubber wedges around the board took the main impact – and nor was there thirty-eight days later, at night, when she again hit something which MacArthur thought might have been a fish or a squid.. Whatever it was initially stuck to the leeward rudder, and MacArthur needed to gybe the boat to lift the rudder out of the water, whereupon the unidentified object fell off.

On her sixth day at sea, MacArthur wrote about the 'fair share of problems' she had had so far, and that while some of them were significant safety issues, others were just part of a never-ending list.

Much later in the voyage, as she was nearing the Equator on her way home, she wrote:

> I rewired both ends of the earth protector for the Active Echo, checked the steering bearings, replaced some protection on the mast, removed the damaged netting protection from the port side, checked all the seals on the float hatches, epoxied the bullseye back on the deck for the Solent and

also bonded the deck that had been torn up as it went flying. Checked the diesel levels too. All OK. You know, the usual Sunday maintenance.

But MacArthur clearly got some pleasure from maintenance work and wrote that she loved looking after *B&Q* even though it could be hard work.

She was also very good at it. 'She is a master fixer with a self-confessed passion for DIY,' *Yachting World* reported during the course of her voyage, 'skilled in the less apparent arts on which ocean races really hinge.'

At the end of her voyage, she paid tribute to her back-up team who designed, built and helped prepare *B&Q*, without whom she would not have completed the voyage with so few problems.

One member of that team was Neil Graham, Offshore Challenge's technical director, who pointed out that:

[Building] reliability into any boat to be sailed single-handed is so important. As the solo sailor, not only do you have to be an expert in every department, but spending time fixing things means you are not sleeping, trimming or navigating which can start a downward spiral chain of events.

Well-Being

Personal Injury

It is not just the boats that are susceptible to damage during such extreme voyages, the sailors are too. In fact, not only are the chances of personal injuries considerably higher than in most people's normal lives, but the chances of receiving outside medical assistance are considerably lower. Essentially solo sailors like Knox-Johnston and MacArthur have to ensure they look after themselves as well as they possibly can.

On Knox-Johnston's ninety-ninth day at sea, when he had just passed the longitude of Cape of Good Hope, his left eye was infected with battery acid. He had been in the engine room checking the batteries with a hydrometer when *Suhaili* broached and he lost his balance. He rushed out on deck where he found that the cockpit was awash, and so he spent about five minutes washing his eye with the sea water conveniently to hand before going below again and continuing the process with fresh water. He added antiseptic eye drops from his medical kit and read in his *Ship Captain's Medical Guide* that

156

the eye should be rested. Over the course of the following week the eye throbbed painfully and it occurred to him that he might permanently lose the use of it. However, 'I was leading and had a slight chance of winning,' he wrote, 'and I felt that this would be worth giving an eye for, so I carried on.' Happily he didn't have to make such a sacrifice, although he did later suffer from a further eye infection caused by the fumes of some disinfectant which leaked into the bilges.

Most of his other injuries were relatively minor. When repairing his spinnaker, he inadvertently sewed his moustache into it and found he had no choice but to jerk his head back to tear himself free. 'It hurt like hell and tears filled my eyes,' he wrote and he then checked in the mirror to reassure himself that the 'symmetry of the moustache was not badly upset.'

He suffered a wrist injury caused by the failure of the brake on his main halyard winch; one morning after a day battling the elements he 'awoke with a stiff back and a bruise the size of a cricket ball at the base of my spine'; various other bruises caused him to later write that he felt as if he had 'just gone through ten rounds with Cassius Clay' (the boxer who later changed his name to Muhammad Ali), and he repeatedly suffered from bruises when he deliberately slept without a bunk board so that if *Suhaili* accidentally gybed while he was sleeping he would be thrown out of his bunk and woken up – 'a very effective alarm'!

He also endured two cooking injuries. The first of these occurred when *Suhaili* lurched just as he was serving hot porridge resulting in 'two blisters the size of half-crowns' on his wrist; and the second was when he was cooking while naked in the tropics, and moved a hot pan from the stove to make room for the kettle and then sat on the pan. For several days afterwards, sitting down caused him great discomfort.

But the biggest threat to his well-being – indeed to his life – began to manifest itself on his 266th day at sea, when he was just three days from crossing the Equator on his way home. 'I do not feel at all well this evening,' he wrote in his log. 'I feel a bit sick and tired and I have a headache. I also have agonising indigestion.' The indigestion worsened and when he consulted his Ship Captain's Medical Guide he was 'really alarmed' as he thought he might have 'anything from appendicitis to stomach ulcers'. He modified his diet and took indigestion tablets but that made little difference. He began to consider his options but as the nearest port was about a thousand miles away – Belem at the mouth of the Amazon – they were few and far between. Just after crossing the Equator he saw a ship heading in the opposite direction. He tried to attract its attention by signalling with his Aldis lam, lighting a hand flare and, conscious of the fact that his life might be at stake, setting off a distress rocket and signalling with his Aldis again. He received the briefest flicker of acknowledgement but his subsequent attempts to communicate were not returned. 'The lousy bastard,' he wrote in his diary. Over the next few days, he saw other ships, two of which passed within half a mile, and none of them answered his signals. He was incensed that so many ships were failing to keep a proper lookout and were ignoring the 'sacred tradition' (not to mention the legal requirement) of going to the aid of other vessels at sea.

After a week or so the symptoms wore off and he came to the conclusion that it had been a 'combination of chronic indigestion and acute imagination' and may have been caused by his supply of tinned bully beef which had probably 'started going off'. 'It shows the dangers of giving a layman a medical book,' he wrote in his log. However, it may have been that his initial diagnosis was terrifyingly accurate. About a year and a half after he completed his voyage, he contracted a definite appendicitis and, after the organ was removed, the doctors told him that they had found some scar tissue indicting that he had previously suffered from the same thing but somehow recovered.

MacArthur too, suffered from her share of injuries although thankfully none were life-threatening. She badly burnt her arm on the generator exhaust while swapping alternator cables from one generator to the other just as B&Q lurched over a wave. She began to suffer from salt sores on her hands and arms early on in her voyage, and later on she had 'white rot' underneath all her fingernails.

On her forty-eighth day at sea the gennaker tack slipped out of the furling gear and hit her on her forehead which caused a far bit of bleeding and left her with a lump.

But her worst injuries occurred on her fifty-fourth day at sea, the day she had to climb the mast twice to repair the damaged mainsail track, just before her homeward path crossed her outward one in the South Atlantic. There was 20 knots of wind at the time and with any movement of the boat greatly exaggerated aloft, MacArthur was thrown repeatedly against the mast while she was up there. During the course of the operation she cut her thumb and she was later amused by the idea that a doctor's advice would be to keep it elevated bearing in mind, she thought with some humour, that she could hardly have had it more elevated than when she was 30m up the mast.

Although she successfully repaired the track, it took its toll on her body and she later wrote about the resulting bruises and aches, and that she was now moving around the boat 'with the speed and elegance of an arthritic robot'.

General Well-Being

'It sounds silly now but in those days no one knew whether a (boat or) human could make it all the way round,' Knox-Johnston wrote several years after his circumnavigation in *Suhaili*. 'We just didn't know about the possible effects of the loneliness. Psychiatrists said a human would go mad.' During the course of his voyage, from time to time he monitored his own mental state to see if there were signs that it was suffering in any way. On his forty-third day at sea he thought he heard voices, and he found this was somewhat disturbing until he realised that the voices were coming from his tape machine, which he had inadvertently left running. He actually found this experience reassuring, in that he had instinctively and immediately recognised that he shouldn't have been hearing voices. 'I am still as sane as I ever was,' he wrote in his logbook.

On 25 August, the *Sunday Mirror* reported on a radio call that Knox-Johnston had made to the paper's reporter in Cape Town:

Robin admits that he sometimes feels 'a bit lonely'. He said 'I usually feel a bit low in the evenings but it cannot be helped. I shall just have to get home quicker. I picked up some music on the radio but this made it even worse. I felt more lonely than ever'.'

With regard to these radio calls that he was able to make in the early part of his voyage, he had very mixed feelings. 'I get excited by getting through,' he wrote in his logbook, 'and then the feeling of anti-climax follows, and I feel depressed.'

Not long after that, he wrote that:

Some of the problems associated with loneliness and having to do absolutely everything for oneself were beginning to appear … I would get restless and long for the voyage to be over and it was not until October that I found I had come to accept at all philosophically that I was to spend perhaps a year of my life in this way.

MacArthur, of course, had considerably less time to get lonely and was also in constant contact with her family and shore team. Despite that, she said at her press conference at the end of her voyage, she had missed the ability to 'look people in the eye'.

The lack of opportunities to get sufficient sleep is a constant and inevitable problem for the solo long-distance sailor. This is particularly true in any sort of race or record attempt when it is essential that the boat always has the right amount of sail up in the prevailing conditions to maximise the speed, without threatening the safety of the boat and crew. MacArthur averaged just five hours' sleep in twenty-four throughout her circumnavigation, and the most she managed in one go was three hours. Not surprisingly this took its toll, and her writings are full of references to her lack of sleep, and that she must try to do something about it. It was the periods of changeable weather conditions – when there was an almost constant need for changes of sail and/or course – that were particularly difficult.

Even when she had the opportunity to sleep it wasn't necessarily that easy to do so, especially in the Southern Ocean, where the motion of the boat was so extreme, and where the noise could be particularly disturbing. She once wrote that *B&Q* foils sometimes produced a whining noise such as one 'you'd expect to hear from a monastery, like a constant ghostly chant.'

MacArthur often slept in *B&Q*'s cuddy, from which she could reach the mainsheet traveller control and headsail sheet in case either needed to be released in an emergency, and with the autopilot control in her hand. 'I was so connected to the boat that I could almost change course whilst dozing,' she wrote.

Everything changed for her as soon as she crossed the finish line and her shore team came aboard and took over the running of the boat. As *B&Q* made her way back to Falmouth that night, MacArthur slept for six hours.

Just over a fortnight into his voyage, Knox-Johnston had settled into a routine. 'I tried to get to sleep at 10pm, if the sailing conditions allowed, and apart from a check at 2 am (more frequently in the shipping lanes or bad weather) I slept through until 6 am.' However, once he got into the Southern Ocean and began to experience regular gales, he found that this routine often had to be abandoned. 'Reducing sail at night to achieve a balance so that I could sleep contributed to the disappointing progress,' he wrote.

His writings often included phrases such as 'I became rather tired and irritable through lack of proper sleep', and 'I want to try to get a full uninterrupted night's sleep if I can as I feel very tired.'

Just before Christmas, when *Suhaili* was about halfway across the Pacific Ocean, she ran into fog in an area where there might well have been icebergs which meant there was 'no thought of real sleep'. For two days, Knox-Johnston kept a lookout, 'cat-napping in the cockpit by day … but staying awake all night staring anxiously into the gloom ahead and imagining all sorts of obstacles looming up.' Once the fog cleared, he took to his bunk and slept for eighteen hours, and on another occasion, having not had an uninterrupted night's sleep for three nights he managed 'twelve beautiful hours sleep and awoke ready for anything.'

It isn't possible to sail around the world from the northern hemisphere by way of the three Great Capes without encountering extremes of temperature: both the heat of the equatorial regions on the outward and homeward passages, and the cold of the Southern Ocean, even during the southern hemisphere summer. While the duration and timing of *Suhaili's* voyage meant that Knox-Johnston was unable to avoid the latter part of the Southern Ocean winter when he first arrived there, *B&Q's* speed ensured that MacArthur had to suffer winter weather in the northern hemisphere at the beginning and end of her circumnavigation.

When she was halfway across the Pacific, MacArthur wrote about the damp weather which 'seeps into your bones' and of how thankful she was that the heat of the generator was drying her thermal clothing which had been soaked several times.

She also wrote about how she managed to sleep in *B&Q's* cuddy in such weather by curling up on her side 'in the foetus position' with her feet constantly wet and cold even in her boots, and how she would try to warm her hands inside a woolly hat while she pulled a blanket over herself.

But the coldest weather she experienced, colder than anything in the Southern Ocean, was when she was just a couple of days from the end of her voyage and a 'freezing northerly wind seemed to be trying to eat right into my soul'.

Knox-Johnston entered the Southern Ocean at the very beginning of September – the equivalent of the beginning of March in the northern hemisphere – and even a week before that he wrote that the 'weather was getting noticeably colder'. Around the same time, in a radio call to the *Daily Mirror*, he had joked: 'if you have a spare helicopter I could do with some dry clothes.' When *Suhaili* was off Otago, New Zealand, on 21 November, Knox-Johnston told the *Sunday Mirror* reporter Bruce Maxwell: 'I cannot stand having wet cold feet. The prospect of another few weeks of it before I reach the Horn is an almost unbearable thought.' About halfway across the Pacific Ocean, *Suhaili* was pooped at a time when Knox-Johnston had left the main hatch open to ventilate the cabin following the spillage of some disinfectant. After spending twenty minutes pumping the bilges, he found that his bedding was completely soaked. 'Although most of my clothing had been damp for months, until this day I had managed to keep my sleeping bag reasonably dry,' he wrote.

Knox-Johnston regularly washed his clothes in a bucket with salt water and detergent, and then rinsed them by trailing them behind *Suhaili* on the end of a piece of rope. If it rained he would also be able to rinse them in fresh water but either way he would hang them on a line in the cabin with the kerosene heater on. However, soon after he rounded Cape Horn he stopped using the heater, as he was concerned about his diminishing supply of kerosene. 'My choice of trousers now lies with the least wet pair,' he wrote and, a bit later, that:

[The] most worn of all my equipment were my clothes ... none of my protective clothing was in good shape. The rubber sea boots were cracking and they leaked ... one advantage was that when they filled with water, it ran out at the foot and I did not have to take them off to empty them.

'I revelled in my new and luxurious state,' wrote Knox-Johnston when *Suhaili* sailed back into a warmer climate. He had a thorough spring clean, which included scrubbing the settee cushions and putting them on deck to air, along with 'everything' else. 'Widow Twankey's laundry never had anything to match my washing line and I reckon I got an extra knot from *Suhaili's* increased windage.'

It is inevitable that the highs and lows experienced by solo sailors such as Knox-Johnston and MacArthur are considerably more extreme than those experienced by the vast majority of leisure sailors, and their writings frequently express this.

'The future does not look particularly bright,' wrote Knox-Johnston on his eighty-seventh day at sea. 'Sitting here being thrown about for the next 150 days … is not an exciting prospect.' He then began to compare his situation with that of an incarcerated criminal:

> A prisoner at Dartmoor doesn't get hard labour like this; the public wouldn't stand for it. And he has company, however uncongenial. In addition he gets dry clothing and undisturbed sleep. I wonder how the crime rate would be affected if people were sentenced to sail around the world alone, instead of going to prison. It's ten months' solitary confinement with hard labour.

At other times, he wrote 'I feel very depressed at the moment and thoroughly frustrated', 'I feel bloody dispirited', and 'I felt very depressed this morning and began wondering why on earth I was punishing myself like this.' Amongst the dreams that Knox-Johnston had during his voyage was a recurring one that he was merely taking part in an eliminating heat and that when it finished he would have to start the proper race. 'I suppose someday I'll read that and laugh,' he wrote, 'but just now … it's a nightmare.'

He often longed for the comforts of home. 'It's about time I made a port,' he wrote soon after entering the Southern Ocean, 'had a long hot bath, a steak with eggs, peas and new potatoes, followed by lemon meringue pie, coffee, Drambuie and a cigar, and then a nice long uninterrupted sleep.' Later in the voyage, he found that:

> [The] soapy smell of a miraculously dry cotton shirt … conjures up memories of a life I have almost completely forgotten, where people daily immerse themselves in special containers filled with hot fresh water – a strange habit which cannot be healthy – sleep in sprung beds with clean white sheets and have special clothes to wear in their beds, and where most peculiar of all, they transfer their food from the cooking pot to a plate before eating.

MacArthur frequently used phrases such as 'running on empty', 'no reserves', and 'digging deeper than ever before.' Three days from the completion of her voyage, she sent an email to her shore team, saying that it was only the energy she felt from other people that was keeping her going, and that the whole experience had been significantly more demanding than the Vendée Globe.

But it was by no means always like that for either of them. 'I can think of no one with whom I'd trade my lot at present,' Knox-Johnston wrote when he was in the South Atlantic on his outward passage. 'Intelligent, attractive and interesting female company is all that I require to make the situation quite perfect.' Soon after he had been thinking of retiring into Melbourne, he wrote: 'thinking of continuing the voyage made my spirits rise immediately'; and when he was off Otago waiting to see Bruce Maxwell he felt 'complete contentment'.

About a week before the end of her circumnavigation, at a time when she knew there was still a significant chance that she might not break the record, MacArthur spoke into her video camera and said how much she loved it out there in the middle of the Atlantic, how happy she was and that she must be 'one of the luckiest people in the world'.

For entertainment, Knox-Johnston enjoyed swimming, music and reading. He took the opportunity to swim whenever the water was warm and calm enough, and this 'kept me cleanly fit!' He enjoyed listening to music on his tape recorder, particularly Gilbert and Sullivan to which he frequently sang along and which 'always cheers me up', but he regretted not taking a tape of 'stirring patriotic stuff'. He describes himself as a 'voracious book reader' and he took over a hundred books with him, including the magnum opus *War and Peace*. As the voyage went on and his supply of unread books diminished, he greatly enjoyed poetry and the mental discipline of learning it. When he rounded Cape Horn and opened the tin containing his Aunt Aileen's fruit cake, his pleasure was enhanced when he saw that there was a piece of the *Times* newspaper inside the tin which gave him 'something new to read as well'.

MacArthur had much less time for entertainment. She took with her a book by the cyclist Lance Armstrong – who, at that time, had been credited with winning the Tour de France six consecutive times before these titles were later revoked for doping offences – but she gave this to Neptune when she crossed the Equator on her outward passage. Soon after passing the Cape of Good Hope, she celebrated *B&Q*'s first birthday with the small bottle of champagne intended for Christmas, and she drew a rosette on an empty envelope and wrote '1 today' on it. 'It sounds silly,' she wrote, 'but that act of celebrating that day brought a huge amount of pleasure to our little world out there.'

On her nineteenth day at sea she wrote about the very limited and carefully planned resources she had on board B&Q: 'I don't have much here really, there are no luxuries – just a few CDs and the odd photo scattered around. But I'm so lucky because the pleasure is inside me, the luxuries are inside me.'

On the last solitary night of her voyage, she played a CD and she 'bopped' and sang along to the music with sheer happiness.

Knox-Johnston's sponsors, the *Sunday Mirror*, arranged for him to visit a psychologist before and after his voyage to ascertain his mental state. On both occasions he was diagnosed as 'distressingly normal'.

Diet

The victualling of a boat for a voyage as long as *Suhaili*'s was a mammoth task, but Knox-Johnston had the advantage of his experience of *Suhaili*'s 1966/67 voyage back from Cape Town.

Most of the food he took was in cans – about 1,500 of them – from which he removed the labels, to prevent them falling off and clogging up the bilges, before marking them with an identification code and then coating them with varnish to minimise rusting. He also took fresh onions and potatoes, and two gross of eggs which were individually coated in grease. By the time *Suhaili* was loaded up, she was floating 2in below her marks. Much to his disappointment, the eggs started going bad after a month, and the onions and potatoes after two. Towards the end of the voyage the contents of the cans started to go off too – typically he found that he had to discard one in every three that he opened – but he still had about three months' supply left when he arrived back in Falmouth. Once he settled into the voyage he ate just two meals a day – breakfast and dinner – and just had coffee and a biscuit for lunch. For dinner he would often make a stew, sometimes two portions so that he could save one for the next evening, when he might add new ingredients to try to give it some variety. In fact, he came to regret the lack of choice, and wished he had spent more time sourcing different varieties of tinned food which were readily available. 'Cooking has become a bind and if I did not have to eat, it would be the first thing I would give up,' he wrote on his thirty-fifth day at sea and, when the voyage was completed, 'I got fed up with the run of stews and bully and baked bean salads, and for several months ate less that I should have done through sheer lack of interest.' In extreme conditions, he made do: on his 115th day at sea in a Force 10, for instance, his dinner consisted of coffee and brandy, half a packet of dates, three handfuls of peanuts, and six digestive biscuits. Throughout the voyage he took vitamin C, calcium and yeast tablets – and wanted to grow mustard and cress to supplement these but decided it would lead to an extravagant use of fresh water – and he attributes the good health he mostly experienced to these.

Knox-Johnston took with him two dozen bottles of spirits and 120 cans of beer. His consumption averaged about a bottle of spirits every sixteen days for most of the voyage but he went for long periods with no alcohol at all, typically having a drink to mark a particular milestone. He also took 3,000 cigarettes which, he later wrote, he could 'well have done without.' He knew they wouldn't last for the whole voyage however, and in his notes that he passed over to the pilot vessel *Wyuna* off Melbourne he wrote:

> I have smoked 1800 to date so at this rate I am going to run out somewhere in the South Atlantic. Spare a thought for me next January when you light up. I'll just be beginning a drastic cure.

As it happens he ran out on 6 March, his 266th day at sea, when he wrote: 'it's a horrible habit anyway.' In October 1969, *The Sunday Times* reviewed his book *A World of My Own* and referred to a moment when he had written about going below for an Irish coffee and a cigarette. 'This is the key to his success,' read the review, 'he had taken tireless precautions without forgetting his creature comforts.'

At various times, *The Sunday Times* reported on the diets of Knox-Johnston's competitors. Ridgway took a 'unique dehydrated balanced diet provided by Horlicks Ltd, individually packed for every day for 400 days'; the two Frenchmen were expected to 'live mainly on rice enlivened by corned beef and onions' while Moitessier would supplement this with 'a litre of wine and three packs of cigarettes a day'; Blyth's supplies included 'an enormous bag of toffees and a large supply of honey'; and King expected 'few comforts in the way of food and no alcohol'.

But it was Nigel Tetley who, encouraged and assisted by his wife, took with him the best quality provisions. His supplies included Scottish octopus, Japanese pheasant and Chinese roast goose, but *The Sunday Times* reported, on 18 May 1969, that many of these delicacies had run out and he was now 'down to the basics of oysters, crab, corned beef, chicken and Irish stew.'

•◆•

MacArthur's victualling was all done by her shore team and the contents were determined by her own previous offshore sailing experience and that of many others. In an interview before she set sail, she told *Yachting World's* Elaine Bunting that:

> I eat purely to survive, I'm not someone who has three mealtimes … I generally eat round the clock to keep my body ticking over. But the food is all packed day by day, the calories are all calculated, and it's calories between cold climates and hot climates which is very important.

Her meals were mostly freeze-dried and, although she tired of their consistent mushiness, she did at least recognise that their quality had improved over the seven years she had been eating them during her ocean voyages. On day twenty-five, she wrote about various dietary problems, in particular that she had gone off porridge and muesli bars, and she lamented the unexpected shortage of olive oil now that she had to share it with the generator.

But she did also have some crackers and cheese, and seventy-one pieces of her mother's 'fantastic flapjack'.

On 26 December, her twenty-ninth day at sea, she wrote in her log about how difficult it was to find time to eat and to sleep, and she referred to the many occasions when she felt she had to choose between one or the other. Three weeks later, on a day of particularly changeable weather conditions, she made herself some lunch but had to go on deck to gybe the boat in 35 knots of wind before she could eat it. She then went back down below and got on to her bunk to try to get some sleep. But then she realised she couldn't remember eating and, sure enough, her lunch was still untouched in the galley. She got up to eat it and then went back to her bunk.

MacArthur had very little alcohol on board but it did include a few small bottles of champagne to mark special moments in the voyage such as the two crossings of the Equator, the rounding of each of the three Great Capes, and Christmas day. The latter, however, was opened a few days early – on *B&Q*'s first birthday – but luckily amongst the Christmas presents from her parents was a tiny bottle of rum.

Nature

Throughout their voyages, Knox-Johnston and MacArthur greatly cherished the natural environment around them. 'People talk about the empty sea and sky,' Knox-Johnston wrote, 'but in my experience, more often than not some form of life is in view.' Storm petrels ('which seem far too fluffy and delicate to live in such a merciless environment') and albatrosses ('one of the most graceful of birds') were the two species of seabirds he saw most of. He also, on one occasion when he was in the Variables, saw two small 'beetle-like insects skipping across the surface of the water' and he wondered how they could possibly survive in such a place.

On her seventeenth morning at sea, MacArthur woke to see four albatrosses circling behind *B&Q* and later wrote that she had 'rediscovered the magic of being out here.' From time to time she wrote with some passion when she saw shearwaters, storm petrels, boobys and albatrosses, and of how they coped with the extreme conditions which they called home.

Just after she rounded the Horn, she saw a lone albatross and had a tear in her eye, as she expected it would be the last one she saw on this voyage but, three days later, she saw another, the biggest she had seen so far. 'It was almost as if it had come to say goodbye to me from the Southern Ocean.'

For Knox-Johnston, it was a school of dolphins that saw him out of the Southern Ocean. They 'gave us a playful welcome as they leapt around the boat, the pilot sitting with a flattened tail on the pressure wave from *Suhaili*'s stem.' In fact, he found that dolphins were regular visitors which he welcomed, but he didn't feel the same way about the whales that he frequently saw, as they could easily have turned *Suhaili* over. However, he 'always felt a little lonely when the whales left; even if we could not communicate, I felt we shared the same difficulties.'

Whales could also have caused considerable damage to *B&Q* and MacArthur was, perhaps, lucky when, on her sixty-second day at sea, *B&Q*'s starboard float passed straight over one.

One of Knox-Johnston's competitors, Bernard Moitessier, had the most extraordinary experience with a school of porpoises when he was sailing south of Stewart Island, off the southern tip of New Zealand's South Island. He was in his cabin when he was distracted by a whistling sound – when he looked outside, he saw that *Joshua* was surrounded by about a hundred porpoises. In particular, he noticed that there were about twenty-five swimming in formation on his starboard side and that they kept veering off to their right in perfect unison. 'I watched wonderstruck,' he later wrote. 'More than ten times they repeat the same thing … I have never seen such perfect ballet.' He thought they, and their companions – 'splashing along in zig-zags, beating the water with their tails, instead of playing with the bow which they usually do' – seemed nervous and he couldn't understand why: until, that is, he looked at his compass and saw that *Joshua* was heading north. Earlier on, the wind had been coming from the west and he had set his wind vane self-steering accordingly to sail a course towards the east. But now, hitherto unknown to him, the wind had backed and was coming from the south, and *Joshua* was heading straight towards the rocks off Stewart Island about 15 miles away. He altered course and headed east again, and immediately the porpoises' behaviour changed. 'Now they play with *Joshua*, fanned out ahead in single file alongside, with the very lithe, very gay movements I have always known.'

The porpoises continued to swim with *Joshua* for a further two hours – considerably longer than the fifteen minutes or so that Moitessier had previously experienced – before all of them, apart from two, left him. Those two stayed with him for a further two hours, one swimming each side of the boat. 'I am sure they were given the order to stay with me until *Joshua* was absolutely out of danger,' Moitessier concluded.

Although Knox-Johnston couldn't have known about that episode until some time afterwards, it is no great surprise that he later wrote that 'being alone in a vast and inhospitable environment gave me a feeling of companionship with any animal'.

MacArthur was often entranced by the sights of the sea and the sky around her as well. 'I'm completely in awe of this place,' she wrote in the early part of the passage across the Southern Ocean. 'The beauty of those immense rolling waves is endless.' She frequently wrote of the 'magnificent' sunsets; and, on her last day in the Southern Ocean, of the vivid lighting effects of the sun behind a rain-filled squall. Even when she fell behind

Joyon's record pace just before crossing the Equator on the homeward stretch, she felt that 'some of the pain was taken away by the most beautiful moon I have ever seen at sea'.

What They Did Next

What MacArthur Did Next

At about 5 p.m. on Monday 7 February 2005, around five hours before *B&Q* crossed the Lizard–Ushant finishing line to claim the solo sound-the-world record, Mark Turner was contacted by Number 10 Downing Street with an offer of a Damehood for Ellen MacArthur. Turner passed the message on to MacArthur who was, according to *The Daily Telegraph*, 'said to have been delighted to accept'. 'Ellen is made a Dame in record time,' read the headline on the newspaper's front page, and certainly in time for one member of the welcoming flotilla to be displaying a 6ft banner saying 'Cornwall congratulates Dame Ellen' as *B&Q* returned to Falmouth.

This caused a certain amount of controversy – 'the only cloud' as the *Telegraph* put it – with some people suggesting it had been rushed through for political reasons. One Tory spokesman said that, although she thoroughly deserved the honour, 'a cynic might suspect that this is not wholly unconnected with the imminence of the general election.' A Labour government spokesman responded by pointing out that Francis Chichester had been knighted after his circumnavigation in 1967. MacArthur's response was that she 'couldn't believe it' and 'felt incredibly privileged'. A short time later, she was also awarded the *Légion d'honneur*, the French equivalent of a Damehood.

Later that year, she received a Laureus Sports Award in the Alternative Sportsperson category, and she was also runner up (to the cricketer Andrew Flintoff who had made a major contribution to the Ashes-winning England team that summer) in the BBC Sports Personality of the Year awards. It was her second time as runner-up in this competition, the first being in 2001, after her Vendée Globe race, when it was won by the footballer David Beckham, who had scored a last-minute goal against Greece to clinch England's place in the 2002 World Cup Finals. She also became, in 2005, the first person to win the Yachtsman of the Year Award three times.

Soon after MacArthur arrived in Falmouth at the end of her record-breaking circumnavigation, she was asked if she might now retire from competitive sailing. She answered:

> No no. This is a nice pause in a good story. There is a lot more that I want to do and I'm not going to stop sailing, that's for sure.

For much of that summer, she was involved in corporate hospitality aboard *B&Q*. She hoped to have another attempt at the transatlantic record and a delivery crew took the boat to New York in readiness for this, but as it turned out the weather refused to cooperate to even allow her to start the voyage.

Seeing her future back in the Open 60 class, in October she set sail from Le Havre with Roland Jourdain in his Open 60 *Sill et Veolia* in the Transat Jaques Vabre, bound for Bahia in Brazil. After leading for much of the race, they were overtaken in the latter stages and in the end they had to settle for second place.

After the race, MacArthur flew back to the UK and barely a fortnight later she was in the air again, this time on her way to the Falkland Islands. From there she sailed on the 120ft aluminium ketch *Tara* – formerly *Seamaster*, the boat on which Peter Blake had been murdered in the Amazon four years earlier – with four others to South Georgia. Once she arrived at this remote island she met up with Sally Poncet, a Southern Ocean environmental expert, and the two of them spent most of the next fortnight together. During this time they carried out an albatross survey on Albatross Island, just off the north-east coast of South Georgia, and the whole experience had a profound effect on MacArthur.

Soon after she returned from South Georgia, *B&Q* was loaded onto a ship and transported to Hong Kong. MacArthur then flew out to Yokohama in Japan to join the boat and from there sailed an eleven-leg voyage with a crew of four to Singapore, and in doing so established an Asian Record Circuit. Along the way she gave talks to school children, businesses and official organisations and, as the company B&Q had opened a number of stores in the Far East, there was clearly a commercial element to the exercise as well. The voyage did, however, mark the end of B&Q's sponsorship of MacArthur's sailing adventures.

Around this time, MacArthur was considering several options for her future: amongst them, competing in the 2007/08 two-handed Barcelona World Race with Roland Jourdain, building a new Open 60 for the 2008/09 Vendee Globe, and even a new career as a rally driver. But since returning from South Georgia, 'something had been gnawing away in my mind,' she wrote. 'It made me stop and think,' she said later in an interview with *The Daily Telegraph*. 'It gave me space and time to see things differently; to realise things I hadn't let into my head before.' As much as anything, it was South Georgia's abandoned whaling stations which had brought home to her the massive issues of sustainability and the finiteness of the world's resources:

> It seemed as though we had just taken what we wanted and moved on. That's what we do.

Furthermore, her own experiences of limited resources in the very specific and relatively small context of her ocean voyages – when she simply had to make do with everything she had on board as there just wasn't anything else available to her – brought the issue home to her even more. 'No experience in my life could have given me a better understanding of the definition of the word "finite",' she said later. 'What we have out there is all we have. There is no more.'

During the summer of 2007, MacArthur took part in just one race – the Round the Island (Isle of Wight) Race in which she skippered an Extreme 40 catamaran with five crew, and in which she won line honours. She spent much of the rest of the summer sailing with the Ellen MacArthur Trust, the charity she had founded in 2003 to take young people recovering from cancer on sailing voyages, to rebuild their confidence and self-esteem.

In November she travelled to Barcelona for the start of the Barcelona World Race. She wasn't competing in it, but the race was organised by her company Ocean Challenges, and so it was entirely appropriate for her to put in an appearance. It was there that she realised the direction her life would now take her:

> Deep down I knew that sailing around the world again would not achieve anything. It wouldn't be helping to find solutions to the problem I was only just beginning to get to grips with … the sailing had given me a voice and my new challenge was to work out the best way to use it.

The day before the race started, 10 November 2007, 'was to be the first day of the rest of my life.'

Almost three years later, after spending a great deal of time visiting power stations, mines and factories, and talking to businesses and government officials, she launched the Ellen MacArthur Foundation. The objective of this organisation was, and is, to promote a circular economy as 'an attractive and viable alternative' to the 'linear "take, make, dispose" economic model' which 'relies on large quantities of cheap, easily accessible materials and energy, and is a model that is reaching its physical limits,' according to the Foundation's website.

> A circular economy is restorative and regenerative by design, and aims to keep products, components, and materials at their highest utility and value at all times … [and is] … a continuous positive development cycle that preserves and enhances natural capital, optimises resource yields, and minimises system risks by managing finite stocks and renewable flows.

'I wasn't looking for this,' she said at the time of the Foundation's launch. 'I didn't want to leave sailing. I just couldn't imagine it. I never thought it would stop for a second … but we have to design a way of not using things up.'

What Knox-Johnston Did Next

On 20 April 1969, two days before *Suhaili* arrived back in Falmouth, Murray Sayle wrote a piece in *The Sunday Times* entitled 'Solo Robin: the surprising hero'. 'It is difficult to see what he can do to cap his tremendous voyage,' the piece concluded, 'but I think we will hear of him again.' Indeed we have.

Although MacArthur and Knox-Johnston were very similar ages at the times of their historic circumnavigations – she was 28 and he celebrated his 30th birthday just over a month before arriving in Falmouth – the contrast between each of their sailing careers before and after those voyages could hardly be more marked. While MacArthur achieved a great deal in the sailing world before her circumnavigation and has done relatively little since, Knox-Johnston's voyage became a very effective springboard for the busy and highly successful sailing career that followed.

Although he was due to return to his job as a Merchant Navy officer with the British India Steam Company, he changed his plans, not least because of various changes that were taking place in the Merchant Navy and a merger of the British India with various other companies. He did, however, continue to serve with the Royal Naval Reserves until 1989.

During the course of 1969, he was presented with various awards, including a CBE, the freedom of the London Borough of Bromley, and the Sicilian town of Riposto's Silver Galleon prize. This was awarded annually to the person judged to have achieved the most daring sea enterprise of the year, and had also been won by Sir Francis Chichester two years earlier.

Knox-Johnston was eventually presented with the Golden Globe trophy at a luncheon on 3 October, a ceremony that had been postponed out of sensitivity towards the Crowhurst family. On receiving the award, he said:

I hope newspapers will continue to sponsor this sort of adventure. It encourages initiative and that, in the long run, must be good for the country … It is nonsense to say newspapers foster irresponsibility by encouraging people into adventures.

The following day, his book *A World of My Own* was published. 'Apart from his competitor, Nigel Tetley, he was presumably the only entrant physically and psychologically equipped to embark on the mad, truly glorious venture,' wrote one reviewer.

In 1970, he won the UK Yachtsman of the Year Award and was presented with the Royal Cruising Club Seamanship Medal. By that time, the next stage of his sailing career was well under way. He and Les Williams had bought an Ocean 71 GRP ketch and named her *Ocean Spirit*, and in 1970 they won the two-man Round Britain and Ireland Race, and then took part in the Middle Sea Race which was organised jointly by the Royal Malta Yacht Club and the Royal Ocean Racing Club. The following year they took line honours, almost a day ahead of the second boat, in the inaugural Cape Town to Rio Race.

In the early 1970s, Knox-Johnston sailed in various RORC races in the UK: in 1971 on Sir Max Aitken's *Crusade*, and then on two of Robin Aisher's Admiral's Cup boats, *Frigate* in 1973 and *Yeoman XX* in 1975.

He was elected as a Younger Brother of Trinity House and as a member of the RNLI Committee of Management in 1972.

In 1973 Rod Macalpine-Downie designed, and Reg White built, the 70ft (21.3m) catamaran *British Oxygen* – at that time the largest racing catamaran in existence – for Knox-Johnston and Gerry Boxall. The following year they won the two-handed Round Britain and Ireland race in her.

Knox-Johnston returned to RORC racing in 1976, this time when he chartered Tony Morgan's *More Opposition*. After a successful season, which included a class win in the non-stop Round Britain race, *More Opposition* won the RORC Class 1 points championship.

Next came Knox-Johnston's second circumnavigation, which would be very different from his first. This time he was taking part in the second Whitbread Round the World Race for fully-crewed boats starting (in August 1977) and finishing in Southampton, with stops in Cape Town, Auckland and Rio de Janeiro. He and Les Williams were joint skippers – Williams on Legs 1 and 3, Knox-Johnston on Legs 2 and 4 – of the 77ft (23.5m) varnished sloop *Condor*. On the first leg, *Condor's* revolutionary carbon fire mast was lost, but she managed to make her way under jury rig to Cape Town, where it was replaced with an aluminium mast. *Condor* then managed to win line honours on Leg 2 (by more than a day) and Leg 4 (by just four hours).

Just over three months later, Knox-Johnston chartered the 80ft (24.4m) ketch *Great Britain II* – also fresh from the Whitbread race – in which he and

Billy King-Harman took part in the 1978 two-handed Round Britain and Ireland Race.

In the early 1980s, Knox-Johnston found himself sailing another 70ft catamaran: *Sea Falcon,* which was effectively an updated, and considerably lighter, version of *British Oxygen.* He sailed her in the two-handed Transatlantic race with King-Harmen in 1981, and the following year he found himself sailing across the Atlantic in her again, but this time with a French crew to whom he had chartered her. Less than a day after arriving in New Orleans, Knox-Johnston and a new crewman set off again to bring *Sea Falcon* back to Plymouth so that he could team up with King-Harman for another two-handed Round Britain race. However, as *Sea Falcon* arrived in Plymouth just seventeen hours before the start of the race, she incurred a time penalty and was hardly in a state of race readiness, and did well to finish in fourth place. Later that year he sailed back across the Atlantic, racing single-handed in the Route de Rhum from Saint-Malo to Guadeloupe. Having established a lead early in the race, his chances of success were dashed when the batteries caught fire and he was forced to stop in Madeira to replace them.

In that same year, the second-ever single-handed round-the-world race began. This was the BOC Challenge (later known as the Around Alone and the Velux 5 Oceans race) which started and finished in Newport, Rhode Island and had stops in Cape Town, Sydney and Rio de Janeiro. Knox-Johnston was the Chairman of the race and he was particularly involved in the subsequent development of the Open 60 Class which has now, for many years, been the predominant monohull class used in single-handed ocean racing.

In 1984, Knox-Johnston sailed another Rod Macalpine-Downie-designed catamaran – the 60 foot (18.3m) *British Airways* – with two crewmen in the inaugural Route del Escrubimenta race, from Spain's Mediterranean coast to Santo Domingo via the Canaries and San Salvador. Mechanical problems led to a failure, amongst other things, of all communications equipment, including the ability to receive weather forecasts and, as a result of this, *British Airways'* crew found themselves having to ride out a hurricane.

The following year, Knox-Johnston and *British Airways* finished third in class in the Round Europe Race, from Kiel to Porto Cervo with six stops, and then won their class in the Monaco to New York race. As a result of this, *British Airways* clinched the 1985 World Championships for 60ft multihulls.

Back on board *British Airways* again in 1986, Knox-Johnston and a crew set a new record of just over seventy-six hours for sailing round Ireland, came fourth with King-Harman in the Round Britain and Ireland Race, and finished second in class with Bernard Gallay in the Carlsberg Two-handed Transatlantic Race from Plymouth to Newport, Rhode Island.

In 1989, Knox-Johnston took part in his sixth Round Britain and Ireland Race, and his first in a monohull since 1970. He and Bob Fisher sailed the 45ft *Barracuda* – the boat which featured in the fictional television drama series *Howard's Way* – to a class win and eleventh place overall.

Throughout this time Knox-Johnston still owned *Suhaili* – and indeed, still does today – and had used her for relatively unadventurous cruising holidays in between his long-distance races. 'She has dominated more than half my life now,' he wrote in *Classic Boat* in 1990, 'and I would feel very lost if I did not think she was lying somewhere nearby, ready, whenever I feel the urge to take off again.' He had felt that urge the previous year, when he sailed her single-handed across the Atlantic in a voyage with a difference: he only used navigation equipment and techniques that had been available in Columbus' time, in the late fifteenth century. His voyage took him via the Canaries to San Salvador in the Bahamas and from there to Norfolk, Virginia. As a result of this voyage he was later awarded the Royal Institute of Navigation's Gold Medal and the Silk Cut Seamanship award. From Norfolk, he and three crew set off to bring *Suhaili* home but they soon found themselves in a storm in mid-Atlantic. *Suhaili* was knocked down four times and eventually lost her masts. A jury rig took her to the Azores, where she was laid up for the winter before new masts were stepped the following spring.

In 1991 Knox-Johnston set sail on *Suhaili* for another unusual voyage, this time with a crew that included the celebrated mountaineer Chris Bonington. They sailed to Kangerlussuaq Fjord – on the east coast of Greenland and just inside the Arctic Circle – from where they attempted to scale a hitherto unclimbed peak, but were defeated by the weather.

The following year, Knox-Johnston became a Freeman of the City of London, and he also took on the role of President of the Sail Training Association – whose topsail schooners *Malcolm Miller* and *Sir Winston Churchill* took countless young people on sail training voyages, and which organises tall ships' races – a position he held until 2011.

The competition for the Jules Verne Trophy was announced in Paris in October 1992. Knox-Johnston, as a member of the Jules Verne committee, was there, and so was Peter Blake. Blake had taken part in all five of the previous Whitbread Round the World races: with Knox-Johnston on *Condor* in the second, and as skipper of *Steinlager* in the fifth, in which he had won all five legs. These two sailing legends agreed to co-skipper a Jules Verne challenge, and so they acquired the 10-year-old 85ft (25.9m) catamaran *Formule Tag*, which they renamed *Enza New Zealand*.

With a total crew of eight, *Enza* crossed the Lizard–Ushant starting line in the early part of 1993, as did two other boats with the same aim. Oliver de Kersausen's trimaran *Charal* started first, followed by *Enza* a few days later, and Bruno Peyron's catamaran *Commodore Explorer* a short time after that.

However, Knox-Johnston and Blake had to abandon their attempt when *Enza New Zealand* collided with something in the Indian Ocean and damaged a hull, and *Charal* also retired. But *Commodore Explorer* – which had overtaken *Enza* just before her retirement – finished the course with less than eighteen hours to spare before the eighty-day time limit expired, and so became the first winner of the Jules Verne Trophy. Various modifications were then carried out to *Enza*, including lengthening her to 92 feet (28.0m), and in January 1994 she set off again. This time she completed the course, and in a time which was more than four days faster than *Commodore Explorer*'s record.

In recognition of this momentous achievement, Knox-Johnston was presented with his second Yachtsman of the Year award, and he and Blake jointly received the inaugural ISAF Sailor of the Year award.

In 1995, Knox-Johnston and Blake were both knighted. Many would argue that Knox-Johnston should have been awarded this honour many years earlier; Chichester received his richly deserved knighthood soon after he completed his one-stop circumnavigation, and few would have quarrelled with Alec Rose's receipt of the same honour at the end of his two-stop circumnavigation. But it did seem an extraordinary oversight that Knox-Johnston – whose first circumnavigation was, by definition, a greater achievement than Chichester's or Rose's – was, at that time, overlooked in this way (although he was awarded the CBE in 1969). *Yachting World* reported in August 1995 that:

The honour, many felt, was long overdue. He is Britain's best-known yachtsman. For apart from his original, epic voyage in *Suhaili*, the world's first solo non-stop circumnavigation, in the wake of Chichester and Rose, both of whom stopped en-route and were knighted, Knox-Johnston has completed virtually every long distance offshore race in the world with some measure of success, including the record breaking Jules Verne with Peter Blake.

It was around that time that another wrong was righted. Soon after, Knox-Johnston stepped ashore at the Royal Cornwall Yacht Club in Falmouth, the club had a commemorative plaque engraved and mounted on the wall next to the steps. However, his name was spelt incorrectly: 'Robin Knox-Johnson'. Unfortunately the error was initially corrected just by modifying the original plaque, but happily it has now been properly replaced with a stone plaque.

In 1996, Knox-Johnston set up the company Clipper Ventures to give ordinary men and women, with or without previous sailing experience, the chance to take part in the Clipper Round the World Race. Each boat would have a professional skipper and all crew members would undergo intensive training before the race began.

In 1997, Knox-Johnston took part in the Atlantic Challenge, a race jointly organised by the New York Yacht Club and the Royal Yacht Squadron, from New York to the Lizard. He was on board the 85ft (25.9m) *Sapphire* which the Royal Yacht Squadron had chartered for the race, but head winds in the latter part of the race, and the need to be back in Cowes punctually, compelled the boat to motor the last stretch.

The following year, Knox-Johnston led another mountaineering expedition to Greenland, again involving Chris Bonington but this time in two of the Clipper 60s.

Around this time Knox-Johnston loaned *Suhaili* to the National Maritime Museum Greenwich. In a letter in *Classic Boat* in June 1999, written to dispel rumours that he had donated his boat to the museum, he explained that her original iron fastenings 'are beginning to fade'. He was keen to renew them but found they were particularly difficult to remove, so he decided to 'allow the fastenings a little longer to decay'. When he received the invitation to display *Suhaili* at the museum, he decided that 'this seemed to provide a neat solution to the problem of where to keep her while awaiting the fastenings' pleasure.' By the summer of 2005, *Suhaili* was sailing again, and Knox-Johnston took her to the Solent to take part in two historic, but friendly, races with *Gipsy Moth IV* and *Lively Lady*. *Gipsy Moth* won line honours in both races while *Lively Lady* – under a handicapping system based on the three boats' average daily mileages during their 1960s circumnavigations – won both on corrected time.

In 2002, Knox-Johnston entered the two-handed Round Britain and Ireland race once again. This time he was sailing in *Spirit*, a 45ft (13.7m) trimaran – it was actually his first time racing a trimaran – with Bill Foster. However, in the early part of the race, *Spirit* was damaged and started to take on water in strong winds and big seas between Land's End and the Isles of Scilly, and retired to Falmouth.

In the conversation between the two solo circumnavigators which *The Sunday Times* reported soon after *Suhaili*'s arrival in Falmouth in April 1969, Robin Knox-Johnston and Francis Chichester expressed a great deal of respect for each other. In particular, Knox-Johnston admired that fact that Chichester had completed his voyage at the age of 65, and he said that if, thirty-five years later, he was fit enough to make a voyage like Chichester's he would be very pleased.

As it turned out, Knox-Johnston began his second solo circumnavigation over thirty-seven years after speaking these words, when he was two and a half years older than Chichester had been when he left Plymouth in *Gipsy Moth IV*. Knox-Johnston's wife Sue had died of cancer in 2003, and it was partly as a result of this tragedy that he decided to enter the race that he had helped to create, and for which his company, Clipper Ventures, was now responsible. The BOC Challenge had been rebranded the Around Alone in 1998 and was now called the Velux 5 Oceans race. In 2006 it would start from Bilbao in Spain and would then have just two stops – in Freemantle, Australia, and Norfolk, Virginia, before returning to Bilbao.

Knox-Johnston's first experience of sailing an Open-class boat had been in an Open 50 with Alex Thomson, a former protégé of his. 'I thought "bloody hell, this is far too dangerous",' he later wrote. 'But I got more and more interested in it and said "I think I can do that. So I'd better do it now before I get too old."' It would be his first solo race since 1988.

Just six months before the start of the race, Knox-Johnston purchased the Open 60 *Fila* in which Giovanni Soldini had won the 1998 Around Alone Race. He renamed her *Saga Insurance* – 'his Saga Insurance sponsorship may raise a smile but it's certainly no joke,' *Yachting World* later reported – and then sailed her across the Atlantic and back as his qualifying passage.

Seven boats started the race in October 2006, but soon afterwards *Saga Insurance* capsized in hurricane force winds and Knox-Johnston was forced to put in to Corunna to repair the damaged mainsail track and instruments. He was in good company, however, as four other competitors also had to return to Spanish ports to repair damage.

Two other British competitors were involved in a dramatic rescue 900 miles south of Cape Town. After the head of the canting keel snapped on Alex Thomson's *Hugo Boss*, the keel began to swing uncontrollably and the boat was taking on water. Mike Golding in *Ecover* was 90 miles ahead of Thomson at the time, and he turned around and sailed upwind towards him. A dramatic but successful rescue followed and, as the two British sailors sailed away on *Ecover*, they watched *Hugo Boss*'s final moments before she sank. More drama followed just six hours later, however, when *Ecover*'s mast snapped. With the race over for both of them, Golding and Thomson built a jury rig and began to make their way slowly to Cape Town.

About a week later, deep in the Southern Ocean – reminiscent of his first circumnavigation when he carried out repairs to his self-steering gear – Knox-Johnston found himself immersed in very cold water trying to free a fishing net in which *Saga Insurance* had become entangled. As it happens, he failed to do so while he was in the water, but managed to find a solution once he was back on board. Despite this, and various problems with electronics, the autopilot and broken sail battens, he arrived in Freemantle in third place. After experiencing a further autopilot failure on his first night at sea at the beginning of the second leg, he returned to Freemantle to fix it before setting off again. During his voyage across the Pacific Ocean he experienced more problems: with his satellite communications systems, for instance, which meant he couldn't download weather information for four weeks, and with his mainsail headboard car which prevented him from fully hoisting the sail. As he rounded Cape Horn two things were repeated from his first passage there thirty-eight years earlier: he wrote 'Yippeeee!' in his logbook and he unwrapped a piece of fruit cake made by his Aunt Aileen – now aged 100 – and wrapped in a page of *The Times* newspaper.

He was keen to resolve his communications and mainsail issues, and so he then sailed in to the Beagle Channel and endured a particularly challenging and miserable passage into Ushuaia. 'Whoever decided that hell had to be hot?' he later wrote. He had now lost a great deal of time – not least because the race rules dictated that he had to spend at least forty-eight hours at each unscheduled stop – but nonetheless he re-joined the race and pressed on to Norfolk and then back to Bilbao and successfully completed the race. Although he was the last finisher, he received widespread praise for his performance throughout the voyage, not least because of his own age but also that of the boat – the oldest and heaviest in the race – which he had never really had time to prepare properly before the start. There was particular admiration for the competitive spirit with which he had approached this adventure, but he said:

> I didn't enter this race just to participate. People often think that life winds down for the over-50s, but this simply isn't true. Life is for living.

As a result of this he became only the second person – Ellen MacArthur had been the other – to win the Yachtsman of the Year award for the third time. Furthermore, in November 2007, to mark the centenary of the formation of the International Yacht Racing Union, Knox-Johnston and MacArthur became two of the first six inductees in the ISAF Hall of Fame, which was created 'to celebrate our heroes across the world, all who have achieved greatness in the sport of sailing.' Amongst the others was Eric Tabarly.

After *Saga Insurance* arrived back in Bilbao, Knox-Johnston made no secret of the fact that he had enjoyed the race, but he added: 'I'm not going to do another solo race. Not bloody likely. There's no point in doing that again.' However, seven years later in the same boat – now renamed *Grey Power* – he entered the Route de Rhum Race from Saint-Malo to Guadeloupe. He found himself feeling more and more competitive during the course of the race in which he finished third, a position with which, he later said, 'I am ecstatic'. When asked why he continued to undertake such voyages he replied: 'While I can, why would I stop? It's what I do.' As a result of this latest achievement, in 2015 he was presented with the Yachtsman of the Year award for a record fourth time.

Meanwhile *Suhaili* was in need of a great deal of work and she was eventually brought back to 'cruising rather than concours condition [over a period of] three years and countless hours', according to Barry Pickthall, writing in *Classic Boat* in 2016. '*Suhaili*'s restoration took longer than it did to build her in the first place.' They removed 1,400 iron fastenings – frustratingly slowly at first, until a technique evolved to make the process less painful – and replaced them with bronze ones; the original iron floors were replaced; the joint between the ballast keel and the wood keel was sealed with glass fibre; the bottom was coated with Coppercoat epoxy antifouling; and her interior joinery was more or less completely replaced. Knox-Johnston wrote in *Classic Boat* that:

> I am very fond of her. She has been part of my life since I was 23. I couldn't imagine life without her, and getting her back sailing is when she is looked after best. She doesn't like going to windward but then neither do I.

Although the interior work was not quite complete, the important parts of the restoration work were finished in time for *Suhaili* to take her place as the guest of honour in a fleet of sixty-five boats in the inaugural Hamble Classic Regatta in September 2016.

What the Other Golden Globe Competitors Did Next

Four of the other Golden Globe competitors did, eventually, achieve their goal of sailing around the world.

However, having missed the opportunity to be the first to circumnavigate solo and non-stop, Chay Blyth wasn't interested in just following in Knox-Johnston's footsteps and so he decided to sail around the 'wrong way', westabout against the prevailing wind and currents. He succeeded in doing this in the purpose-built 59ft (18m) ketch *British Steel*, completing the voyage in August 1971 after 292 days at sea. He circumnavigated twice more but each time with a crew and with stops, in the Whitbread Round the World Races of 1973/74 and 1981/82. His other sailing exploits included Round Britain and Transatlantic races, and in 1984 he capsized his trimaran off Cape Horn while attempting the New York to San Francisco record. After nineteen hours in the water, he and his crew were rescued by a passing fishing boat.

In 1992, he formed the company Challenge Business to organise round-the-world races, giving ordinary men and woman, with or without previous sailing experience, the opportunity to take part under the command of a professional skipper (just as Knox-Johnston's Clipper races would do subsequently).

John Ridgway founded the Ridgway Adventure School at Ardmore in the early 1970s and it has been run by him and his family ever since. He, too, has taken part in the Whitbread Round the World Race, in his 57ft (17.3m) ketch *English Rose VI* in 1977/78, and he has sailed the same boat around the world twice more: two-handed non-stop in 1983/4 and with his family on a multi-stop voyage from 1993 to 1995. He has also undertaken a number of other sailing, canoeing, climbing and exploration adventures.

Bill King attempted a solo circumnavigation twice more in *Galway Blazer II*. In 1971, the boat was holed when she collided with a submerged object off the coast of Australia, but somehow King made it safely to Freemantle, 400 miles away. He finally achieved his goal two years later. He wrote a number of books about his World War Two and sailing experiences, and at the age of 78 he took up hang gliding. He was the last surviving British Second World War submarine commander when he died in 2012 at the age of 102.

Loick Fougeron also needed another two attempts before achieving his circumnavigation goal. In 1972, he was forced to abandon his two-man voyage on board his 39ft (12m) ketch *Captain Browne II*, but four years later, on the same boat, he successfully circumnavigated alone. He died in February 2013 at the age of 86.

After arriving in Tahiti in June 1969, Bernard Moitessier spent two years there, during which time he took a mistress and fathered a son. He then set sail again in *Joshua*, but in 1982 she was wrecked when she dragged her anchor off the west coast of Mexico. She was rescued, however, and Moitessier then gave her to a local man (although some reports suggest he sold her for $20) who restored her. Since 1990, she has been in the care of the French National Maritime Museum in La Rochelle.

Moitessier himself, meanwhile, became a political activist and eventually returned to Paris to write his autobiography. He died of prostate cancer in June 1994 at the age of 69.

Alex Carozzo operated *Gancia Americano* as a charter boat until he sold her in 1974. She is now thought to be in Costa Rica or Panama. In 1990, Carozzo sailed *Zentime* – a 6m converted GRP engineless lifeboat to which he added a gaff cutter rig – from Gran Canaria to San Salvador, a voyage which took him forty days. At the time of writing in the autumn of 2017, he was in the process of completing the build of a 9.6m plywood boat with a cutter rig which he hoped to sail, at the age of 85, from Venice to the Galapagos Islands.

After coming so close to completing his voyage in 1969, Nigel Tetley was desperate to try again. He was awarded a £1,000 consolation prize by *The Sunday Times* and he commissioned a new 60ft (18.3m) trimaran, *Miss Vicky*, but was unable to raise the funds to complete her. In February 1972 he went missing, and three days later he was found hanging from a tree in the woods near Dover.

More Record-Breaking

'As Sir Roger Bannister discovered,' wrote Paul Heywood in *The Daily Telegraph* soon after MacArthur completed her circumnavigation, 'A new record time is merely an impermanent line in the wet sand of human achievement.' *Yachting World*'s editor Andrew Bray thought, however, that 'it will take a supreme effort for anyone to better it this time'.

At the end of 2007, two Frenchman – Francis Joyon, from whom MacArthur had taken the record, and Thomas Colville – were preparing to attempt to do just that. Colville had previously raced around the world twice: with Olivier de Kersauson in his successful attempt at the Jules Verne record in 1997, and in the 2000/01 Vendée Globe, in which he came sixth. Joyon's original *IDEC* had been wrecked when he was sailing her back across the Atlantic and he overslept just as he was nearing the French coast, and so he had a new Nigel Irens-designed trimaran, as did Colville.

Joyon's new *IDEC* was 97ft long (29.9m) and was built by Marsaudon Composites in Brittany, and Colville's 105ft (32.0m) *Sodeb'O* was built by the same company that had produced *B&Q* – Boatspeed in Sydney, Australia – and was christened by Ellen MacArthur.

Just before the two boats set off, *Yachting World*'s Elaine Bunting wrote that MacArthur's record 'will eventually be broken' and MacArthur herself agreed:

> Yes, the record's beatable, and I'm sure one of them will break it this winter. *IDEC* and *Sodeb'O* are both bigger boats so in theory they'll be faster … it's likely but it's not a dead cert. You've got to get that boat round the world.

IDEC set off in November – and 'got off to a blistering start, covering 425 miles during his first twenty-four hours at sea,' according to *Yachting World* – and *Sodeb'O* followed early in the new year. However, Colville was forced to retire in the Indian Ocean after *Sodeb'O* was damaged following a collision, very probably with ice. He had just set a solo twenty-four-hour record of 619 miles.

Joyon, however, had better luck and returned to the Lizard–Ushant finishing line after just 57 days 13 hours 34 minutes and 6 seconds, beating MacArthur's record by just over a fortnight. 'Joyon the Incredible,' read the headline on the front page of *Yachting World*. In setting his 2004 record he declined to use the services of a weather router, but this time he put 'instinct and experience over data and science and was happy to act on weather advice from Jean Yves Bernot rather than waste hours poring over GRIB files,' *Yachting World* reported. *IDEC*'s systems were powered entirely by solar and wind energy, so this was the first non-stop circumnavigation record to be set without using any fossil fuel. In the Southern Ocean the weather systems at one point forced him down as far as 59-degrees South, where he saw five icebergs in one day – this, he thought, was 'beginning to get a bit worrying'. On the way back up the Atlantic, he had to climb the mast to deal with a problem with the main halyard sheave and while he was there he noticed that a shroud terminal had worked loose. He thought that this would spell the end of the record attempt but a few days later he was able to fix it and press on. At that time only one boat – the 124ft (37.8m) catamaran *Orange II* which had a crew of twelve – had ever sailed around the world faster.

'I can imagine how this record could be done in fifty days,' Joyon said afterwards, 'but I will not be the one who tries. From now on I am going to take care of my wife and children.'

'But that's what he said last time,' wrote Bunting.

At the end of 2008 – with the damaged *Sodeb'O* repaired – Colville set off on another attempt. This time he completed the course in the time of 59 days 20 hours, 47 minutes and 43 seconds, comfortably beating MacArthur's time but an agonising two days slower than Joyon's new record.

Undeterred (and having circumnavigated as part of the winning Jules Verne crew on the trimaran *Groupama 3* in 2010) he began another attempt in January 2011, but this time he was slower than his own previous time, finishing in 61 days 7 minutes and 32 seconds. Ironically, however, he had sailed at an average speed which was 0.31 knots faster than Joyon had done three years earlier, but weather conditions had forced him to take a less direct route, and he had sailed more than 2,000 miles further.

He won another round-the-world trophy for crewed boats in 2011/12 when he sailed on the Volvo Open 70 Groupama in the Volvo Ocean Race, and in November 2013 he was ready for another solo attempt. However, he had to abandon this one after little more than a day, having damaged his pulpit. It was very quickly repaired, but he then had to spend two months on standby for another attempt. On 17 January 2014, *Sodeb'O* crossed the Lizard–Ushant line for the last time. Just two weeks later, having made slow progress down the South Atlantic and with an unfavourable forecast for the first part of the Indian Ocean, Colville decided to abort this attempt and return to France.

He then decided that for his next attempt he would sail a different boat. He acquired Olivier de Kersausen's trimaran *Geronimo* which had won the Jules Verne Trophy in 2004 and, with input from specialist multihull designers VPLP, set about radically converting her, not least to allow him to sail her single-handed. This included building a new main hull and a new rig, and fitting new foils which had come from Oracle Team USA's 2010 America's Cup winning boat. The converted boat – 5 tonnes lighter than *Geronimo* had been – was renamed *Sodebo Ultim*.

Colville set sail on 6 November 2016. By the time he crossed the Equator he was 250 miles ahead of Joyon's record, and he doubled that when he passed the longitude of the Cape of Good Hope and continued to increase his lead from there. At Cape Horn he was four days ahead. He eventually arrived back in Brest on Christmas Day having annihilated Joyon's record by completing the course in 49 days 3 hours 7 minutes and 38 seconds, at an average speed of 24.1 knots. He said soon afterwards:

Great dreams never come off first time. I failed, I fell, I picked myself up again, I rebuilt myself.

Francis Joyon may have lost his solo record but, on the day that Colville finished, he was a week into an attempt to win the Jules Verne Trophy on the trimaran *IDEC SPORT* with five crew members. *IDEC SPORT* – as *Groupama III* – had previously had three attempts to win this trophy with her then-skipper Franck Cammas. The first time, in 2008, she had capsized when one of her floats broke off but, amazingly, she was within helicopter range of New Zealand and all the crew were rescued very quickly. A year later, after she had been salvaged and repaired, less drastic structural damage forced her to retire off the Cape of Good Hope, but in 2010 (with Thomas Colville amongst the crew) she completed the voyage in a record time of 48 days 7 hours 44 minutes 52 seconds. But two years later, Loick Peyron's *Banque Populaire V* brought the time down to 45 days 13 hours 42 minutes and 53 seconds, and that was the time Joyon and his crew were now trying to beat. Joyon may well have hoped to hold both the solo and fully-crewed records simultaneously but at least, after holding neither for a month and a day, he had one of them: *IDEC SPORT* finished on 26 January in a time of 40 days 23 hours 30 minutes and 30 seconds.

Slightly less than a year after Colville finally managed to beat the solo record, it was broken again – by another Frenchman, François Gabart sailing the 98ft trimaran *Macif*. Gabart had established himself as a highly accomplished solo sailor when he won the 2013/14 Vendee Globe in a then-record time for the race. But beating the solo record in 2017 took his standing to another level altogether, partly because he did it at his first attempt but also due to the margin by which he did it: he finished after just 42 days 16 hours and 40 minutes. He reached Cape Horn after just twenty-nine days which was faster than any previous boat, fully crewed or otherwise; he set a new solo 24-hour record of 851 miles, an average of 35.2 knots; his fastest speed was 47 knots; and his average speed all the way round the world was an astonishing 27.2 knots.

The 2004 headline question 'can this record be beaten?' seems almost absurd now that it has been, four times and now by more than thirty days. To ask the same question again now might seem to be much more valid, but at the same time still a little risky.

The French Connection

It was the thought that the French sailor Eric Tabarly might be considering a solo non-stop circumnavigation that first motivated the fiercely-patriotic Robin Knox-Johnston to attempt the voyage himself. Perhaps this was effectively the beginning of the French–British rivalry in the sport of single-handed ocean racing that endures to this day. At that time, the tally between the two countries was pretty level: Chichester had won the first single-handed transatlantic race (in 1960) and Tabarly had won the second (in 1964). Knox-Johnston well remembered the accolades Tabarly had received in the French press after his victory:

> [The] inference being that the Island Race had been proved inferior seamen to the French. That made my blood boil at the time and I could picture the headlines if Tabarly became the first person to sail right round the word non-stop. We'd never hear the last of it. By rights a Briton should do it first.

When writing about *Suhaili*'s circumnavigation in his book *A World of My Own*, Knox-Johnston's patriotism often comes to the fore. On his fifty-third day at sea he was listening to Gilbert and Sullivan on his tape recorder. 'It always cheers me up but I would have liked a tape of stirring patriotic stuff – the thought of generations of Britons and their achievements always encourages me.' In early December, when he was frustrated by unfavourable winds he wrote: 'If the French are meant to win – OK, but there is no need to torture me as well as allowing me to lose.' And, a short time later, when he had yet more unfavourable winds:

> When I get home I shall feel like a man who has run 100 yards in 20 seconds in the Olympic Games. Poor old Britain, she has a poor enough champion in the race as it is, but even our best could not do much better in these conditions. Drake and Nelson must be weeping.

On his 256th day at sea, when he was in the South Atlantic and on his way home, he heard something on the radio about a diplomatic row between France's President de Gaulle and the British Ambassador to France. 'I awoke full of indignation,' he wrote in his log. In fact this motivated him to leave his big headsail up when he saw a squall approaching, as a result of which he calculated that he had sailed an extra 5 miles that he wouldn't have otherwise covered. 'I don't think the five miles will affect the issue of the race somehow, and I cannot see de Gaulle being tumbled from office by it, but it made me feel better.'

Tabarly, of course, never attempted a solo circumnavigation, but for almost the whole of Knox-Johnston's voyage his perceived main rival was the other Frenchman, Bernard Moitessier. After *The Sunday Times* learnt of Moitessier's retirement it reported that:

> [His] turn-about has shocked his wife and a growing number of admiring Frenchman. A 'national decoration' was planned for him, possibly the *Légion d'honneur*. And a massive escort of French yachtsmen – even, it was expected, the French navy – was planned for his return to France.

Chichester shared Knox-Johnston's patriotism. 'Robin has put up a tremendous performance,' he said soon after *Suhaili* arrived back in Falmouth, 'and I, for one, am proud that he is a fellow Englishman.'

In the ongoing single-handed transatlantic races, the pendulum swung briefly back towards the British. In the 1968 race, things went badly for Eric Tabarly from the start: on the second day he was in collision with a freighter, as a result of which *Pen Duick* suffered damage to her mast and to one of the floats, and he put back into Plymouth for repairs. When he set off again, he found that there was excess vibration in the rudder and so he took her into Newlyn. Setting off from there again he found the problem persisted and so he retired.

Meanwhile, Geoffrey Williams, sailing the 57-foot (17.4m) ketch *Sir Thomas Lipton*, led the thirty-five-boat fleet into Newport, Rhode Island, and was one of five British sailors – including Knox-Johnston's then-future co-skipper Leslie Williams in fourth place – to beat the leading Frenchman, who was ninth.

However, six of the next seven solo transatlantic races were won by French sailors (the exception was in 1980 when an American won it) with Tabarly prevailing again in 1976. In 2000, for the first time, there were two classes – multihulls and monohulls – and this allowed the spoils to be shared between Francis Joyon and Ellen MacArthur; and four years later between Michel Desjoyeaux and Mike Golding.

The Vendée Globe has been almost completely dominated by the French, both in terms of both participation and success. A total of 166 boats have started the eight races held so far, and 105 of those have been sailed by French skippers; of the 88 boats that have completed these races, 58 have been French; every race has been won by a French sailor and 12 out of the 16 other podium places have been occupied by the French.

The first British sailor to finish the Vendée Globe was Pete Goss, in the third race (and famously rescuing the Frenchman Raphael Dinelli along the way), and it is almost true to say that there has been a British sailor on the podium in every race since then. Ellen MacArthur was second in 2001 and Mike Golding was third four years later. In 2009, Sam Davies was the third sailor to arrive back in Les Sables d'Olonne but was officially placed fourth after the French sailor who finished behind her was, quite rightly, given redress having gone to the aid of another boat. British sailors also finished in fifth, sixth and eighth place that year. Alex Thomson achieved podium places in both of the last two races: third in 2013 and, after a nail-biting pursuit of the leader all the way back up the Atlantic, second in 2017.

The eight BOC Challenge/Around Alone/Velux 5 Oceans races held to date have had a total of six French class winners, and ten of other nationalities, but none from Britain.

•◆•

In 1997 Ellen MacArthur spent three months in France and, according to *Yachting World*, learnt 'passable French'. She subsequently became fluent and it wasn't long before the French people took her to their hearts to the extent that when she finished the Vendée Globe in 2001 an estimated 200,000 people were in Les Sables d'Olonne to greet her, twice as many as had met Michel Desjoyeaux, the French winner of the race, the day before. When Desjoyeaux was asked about MacArthur's fame and popularity in the UK he said: 'I think it is like Eric Tabarly in France in 1964 and the passion for sailing by the French people that he ignited when he won the OSTAR.'

When MacArthur broke the solo non-stop round-the-world record in February 2005, two of Britain's leading national newspapers had different takes on the reaction of Francis Joyon, the previous holder. 'Perhaps a little irritated at his record falling so soon,' wrote Richard Alleyne in *The Daily Telegraph*, 'the Frenchman is reported to be spending February alone on his boat.' *The Times*, meanwhile, quoted Joyon graciously saying:

> I always said that Ellen was a serious contender and I can see today that she has decided to prove me right. The mere fact that she was able to sail round the world non-stop was quite an exploit, but to smash the record at the same time fully deserves my warmest congratulations.

The *Daily Telegraph*'s Colin Randall thought that MacArthur had 'won a place to precious in the hearts of the French that she is probably the only living Briton they do not mind losing to,' and he backed that up by reporting on some of the praise in the French press: *Le Parisien* called her 'Queen Ellen', *Le Figaro* the 'legend of the seas', and *France Soir* 'an immense slip of a girl who took on oceans that gave no respite, and conquered them.'

Robin Knox-Johnston was full of praise for, and pride in, MacArthur's achievement:

How long this record will last I don't know. I expect the French are already planning to beat it. I think they are going to find it hard. Isn't it nice we have a Brit doing it for once?

And to MacArthur herself, he said:

It is an amazing achievement and we are all immensely proud of you. You have put us back on the sailing map.

He was right, of course, about the French plans: it wasn't long before there were further record attempts, but not just by one Frenchman but by three. And their respective achievements are simply extraordinary: in fact, the only things more astonishing than the margin by which Joyon beat MacArthur's record in 2008, were the margins by which Colville and Gabart have beaten the record since.

Other Round-The-World Races

When Murray Sale and Ron Hall of *The Sunday Times* compiled the rules for the Golden Globe race, they sensibly decided to allow flexibility with regard to starting and finishing ports to allow competitors to stick to plans they had already made. As part of the race announcement on 17 March 1968, there was an explanation regarding this part of the rules:

> There has been some discussion as to what constitutes a circumnavigation. The easiest way round the world by sail is in the southern hemisphere. Hobart to Hobart, for instance, is nearly 14,000 miles shorter than Plymouth to Plymouth. The only way to equalise this huge difference is the requirement that to qualify for the Golden Globe, yachtsmen should set out from a northern latitude. Similarly, to qualify for the £5,000 prize – which depends on the precise time the voyage takes – it was thought

fairer that the yachtsmen should all cover the same distance and so the British mainland has been selected as a convenient starting point. Foreign boats and sailors will be more than welcome to come to a British port to join in.

The words 'the same distance' could be called into question. On a completed circumnavigation, Blyth's chosen port of Hamble would have involved a good 300 miles more sailing than Falmouth, for instance. All but one of the other competitors started from ports between these two, the exception being Ridgway, whose favoured port of Inishmore in theory would have involved even less sailing than Falmouth. However, he is thought to have chosen Inishmore for emotional, rather than tactical, reasons and, at the time he made his decision, he knew that it contravened the rules for the £5,000 prize. It was only later that a new *Sunday Times* ruling legitimised his choice.

The fact that there was only one finisher in the Golden Globe race negates the need for any controversy with regard to these different distances, but it could have been so different if two competitors had completed their voyages very close together (in the case of the Golden Globe trophy) or two had done so in very similar elapsed times (in the case of the cash prize).

After the Golden Globe, it was thirteen years before there was another single-handed race around the world, and a further seven before there was a non-stop race. The BOC Challenge race – with Robin Knox-Johnston as its chairman – first took place in 1982, starting and finishing in Charlestown, USA with stopovers in Cape Town, Auckland and Punta del Este. It then took place at four-yearly intervals up until 2010/11, and has also been known as the Around Alone and the Velux 5 Oceans. Ports on the east coast of America were chosen for the start and finish of the first five races before moving to Spain and then to La Rochelle, France. The route has always been eastabout and via the three great capes.

After winning the first two BOC Challenges, Frenchman Philippe Jeantot felt that a non-stop race would be more worthwhile and so he founded the Vendée Globe Challenge. The first race started in November 1989, the second in 1992, and it has subsequently been held every four years. Jeantot chose his own home port – Les Sables d'Olonne on the west coast of France – for the start and finish, and it has remained there ever since. The route for this race, too, has always been eastabout and via the three great capes. In all bar the second race, the winning time has broken the existing record, which now stands at just over 74 days and 3 hours (set by Armel de Cléac'h in 2016/17) which is barely a day longer than Francis Joyon's 2004 multihull record.

The first fully-crewed round-the-world race – the Whitbread Round the World Race, now the Volvo Ocean Race – started in 1973, and twelve races have been completed to date, with the thirteenth due to end in June 2018. The first seven races started and finished in the Solent, and the eighth started there too, but the event then moved further afield with starts in Vigo and Alicante, and finishes in Gothenburg, St Petersburg, Galway and The Hague. The routes have all been eastabout and have all included a rounding of Cape Horn. The first nine races maximised the Southern Ocean element, but in the 2008/9 race the route was around the top of Australia visiting India, Singapore and China. Since then the race has included stops in the Middle East and/or the Far East. In the first three races there were just three stopovers but this number has gradually increased and there have been eight or more in each race since 1997. There were twelve in 2011/12 – but this included four additional ones to allow the fleet to be transported on cargo ships through an area with a significant pirate threat. In total, forty-four ports have now been used for starts, stopovers and finishes.

It is perhaps no coincidence that the two versions of round-the-world races in which a professional skipper leads a crew of ordinary men and woman, some of whom have no previous sailing experience, were founded by Golden Globe competitors. Chay Blyth's Challenge Business ran four editions of a race – sequentially known as the British Steel Challenge, the BT Global Challenge, and the Global Challenge – between 1992 and 2005 before it got into financial difficulties. These races started and finished in Solent ports and followed a 'wrong way' westabout route, similar to Blyth's own 1970/71 solo circumnavigation but with stops.

Ten editions of Robin Knox-Johnston's Clipper Race have been completed to date, and another started in August 2017. All have used British ports for their starts and finishes and have generally followed trade wind routes. The races have had a varying number of stopovers but typically around fifteen, and all of them have taken the fleets through the Panama Canal. The first four races used eight Clipper 60s – based on the David Pedrick-designed Nicholson 58 – and followed a westabout route; the next four races went eastabout in a fleet of ten Ed Dubois-designed Clipper 68s; and then eastabout again in twelve Tony Castro-designed Clipper 70s. Around 2,000 people have taken part in these races to date.

There have been just two fully-crewed non-stop round-the-world races, each of them eastabout and via the three great capes: The Race, which started (on New Year's Eve 2000) and finished in Barcelona;; and the 2005 Oryx Quest which started and finished in Qatar in the Middle East.

There have been three editions of the two-handed eastabout Barcelona World Race which, as its name suggests, starts and finishes in Barcelona. These have all been non-stop races, but the next one, which starts in January 2019, will have a stopover in Sydney.

Races around the planet could start and finish from almost anywhere. But, it would seem, the starting and finishing ports for most round-the-world races have been largely determined by Sir Francis Chichester, *The Sunday Times* and the subsequent dominance of the French in the field of circumnavigations. Of the forty-eight races mentioned above, twenty-two have started and twenty-one have finished in the UK; six have finished in other parts of northern Europe; nine have started and finished on the French Atlantic coast; and eight have started and four have finished on the European Mediterranean coast.

Outside of official races are the record attempts. In 1972, the International Yacht Racing Union (subsequently the International Sailing Federation and now World Sailing) established the World Sailing Speed Record Council (WSSRC), initially to monitor high-speed records, normally over a distance of just 500m. But in 1988, the WSSRC's responsibilities were extended to include long-distance records, including round-the-world attempts.

At that point, the WSSRC formulated the following rule, which deliberately allows the flexibility for a variety of different starting and finish points to be used:

> To sail around the World, a vessel must start from and return to the same point, must cross all meridians of longitude and must cross the Equator. It may cross some but not all meridians more than once (i.e. two roundings of Antarctica do not count). The shortest orthodromic track of the vessel must be at least 21,600 nautical miles in length calculated based on a 'perfect sphere'. In calculating this distance, it is to be assumed that the vessel will sail around Antarctica in latitude 63-degrees South.

When the Jules Verne Trophy was established in 1992, the rules dictated that the start and finish line would be between Créac'h lighthouse on Ushant Island in France and the Lizard Lighthouse in the UK. This not only fitted in with the WSSRC's rules, but would also be convenient for the French: amongst the nine winners of the trophy and eighteen failed attempts to date, all but four have been skippered by French sailors. The fact that twice as many have failed to win the trophy as have succeeded – due to gear failure, collision or just sailing too slowly – is highly significant: it is, quite simply, astonishingly difficult to beat the ever-decreasing times set by the trophy winners. Bruno Peyron was the first Jules Verne winner – in a time of just over 79 days and 6 hours in 1993 – and the rate at which the record has been reduced since then is extraordinary. Francis Joyon and his crew's current record of a little less than 41 days is barely more than half the original target time. Robin Knox-Johnston and Peter Blake remain the only non-French winners of the trophy.

In the case of the single-handed record attempts, the WSSRC's is the only rule with which it is necessary to comply, but clearly it makes complete sense for them to use the Jules Verne Ushant–Lizard line, not least to facilitate public understanding, especially because the leading protagonists – MacArthur, Joyon, Colville and Gabart – come from the countries at each end of that line.

The 2018/19 Golden Globe

On 1 July 2018, a new round-the-world solo non-stop race will start in Les Sables d'Olonne. This will be the 2018/19 Golden Globe Race, which will commemorate the fiftieth anniversary of the original race. However, unlike any of the ocean races held for many years, entrants will only be allowed to use similar boats and items of equipment to those available to the 1968 competitors.

To take part, all boats must:

Be between 32ft and 36ft (9.75m – 10.97m)
Be designed before 1988,
Have a rudder hung from the trailing edge of a long keel
Have a minimum displacement of 6,200kg

Competitors will not be allowed to use any electronic navigation aids, and will not be able to use any shore-based weather routing services. They will, however, carry some electronics for use in an emergency and for regular and regulated communication with the race organisers.

Many people thought that this race should start and finish in Falmouth, in recognition of the fact that it was the chosen port of the only finisher in the original race. However, Plymouth was initially selected as the host port, before difficulties in securing sponsorship (possibly as a result of the UK's decision to leave the European Union) resulted in a move to Les Sables.

The course will naturally be eastabout via the three great capes, but it will also, largely for safety reasons, include restrictions on the latitude below which boats can sail in the Southern Ocean and with a number of compulsory gates. Four of these gates are intended to allow competitors to rendezvous with other vessels and talk to the press, family and friends, and also hand over film, letters and logbooks just as the 1968/69 sailors did. Similarly, the 2018/19 competitors will not be allowed to receive any items from these other vessels.

On 14 June 2018 – the exact fiftieth anniversary of the day that Knox-Johnston began his circumnavigation – the competing boats will take part in a parade of sail around Falmouth Harbour – expectedly along with *Suhaili*, *Joshua*, *Gipsy Moth IV* and *Lively Lady* – before making their way to Les Sables for the start of the race just over a fortnight later. All competitors who reach the Les Sables finish line before 3 p.m. on 22 April 2019 – the exact fiftieth anniversary of *Suhaili*'s finish – will receive a *Suhaili* trophy, and the official prize-giving will take place that evening.

The race was the idea of Australian Don McIntyre who himself took part in the 1990/91 BOC Challenge and recognised that over the years round-the-world races had become 'increasingly performance orientated, sailed by elite sportsmen and women in ever more extreme yachts, focused on winning at all costs.' While conceding that there was 'nothing wrong with that' he wanted to organise a race 'where adventure takes precedence over winning at all costs'. A big part of his initial motivation for doing so was that he wanted to compete in it himself, but he soon realised that it was going to grow into a much bigger and more successful event than he initially imagined, and so he decided to concentrate on its organisation.

The race is limited to thirty entries, and it is highly likely that at least twenty boats will cross the start line on 1 July. It is expected that the competitors will come from at least a dozen countries of which France, perhaps not surprisingly, will be the best represented.. Inevitably their levels of experience will vary significantly, but all of them will be considerably more experienced, and prepared, than most of the 1968 competitors. Apart from anything else, they are required to have sailed at least 10,000 miles – 2,000 of which must be solo – before the race start. Of those who are expected to take part, ten have previously sailed around the world in various ways and in generally much faster boats, including the Whitbread or Volvo race, the Vendée Globe, the Jules Verne and the BOC Challenge. The most experienced competitor is likely to be Jean-Luc van den Heede, a five-time solo circumnavigator and the current holder of the westabout solo record.

The most popular boats will be the Rustler 36 (seven are expected to start the race), the Biscay 36 (four) and the Endurance 35 (four). One competitor – Abhilash Tomy from India – is expected to take part in a near replica of *Suhaili* which will have been built, just like her predecessor, in India. Tomy's boat, however, has not been built traditionally, but is a lighter wood/epoxy version.

Such is the positive response in the world of sailing to the 2018/19 Golden Globe, that McIntyre is already planning another race to take place four years later. He hopes to take part in that one himself.

In a further development, it is planned to build ten replicas of *Joshua* – in steel just as the original boat is – to form a '*Joshua* Class'. They will start a few weeks after the smaller '*Suhaili* Class', which will be open to the same type of boats as the 2018/19 race. The idea behind this is to try to deliberately recreate the pursuit race feel which, although unintentional in 1968/69, did promote excitement and speculation as to the likely winner up until it became apparent that Moitessier had retired. This will never resolve the argument as to whether *Joshua* would have arrived back in Plymouth before *Suhaili* reached Falmouth in 1969, but it will certainly add to the debate.

Bibliography

Classic Boat
Sunday Mirror
Falmouth Packet
Mirror
The Daily Telegraph
The Sunday Times
The Times
The West Briton
Yachting Monthly
Yachting World
Yachts and Yachting

Chichester, Francis, *Gipsy Moth Circles the World* (London: Pan Books Ltd 1969)
Chichester, Francis, *The Lonely Sea and the Sky* (London: Hodder and Stoughton Ltd 1964)

Eakin, Chris, *A Race Too Far* (London: Ebury Press/Random House 2009)

Knox-Johnston, Robin, *A World Of My Own* (London: Corgi 1971)

MacArthur, Ellen, *Full Circle* (London: Michael Joseph/Penguin 2010)

MacArthur, Ellen, *Race Against Time* (London: Michael Joseph/Penguin 2005)

Moitessier, Bernard, *The Long Way* (London: Adlard Coles Ltd 1974)

Nichols, Peter, *A Voyage For Madmen* (London: Profile Books Ltd 2002)

Ridgway, John, *Round the World with Ridgway* (London: William Heinemann Ltd 1978)

Slocum, Joshua, *Sailing Alone Around the World* (London: Adlard Coles Nautical 1997)

Tomalin, Nicholas and Hall, Ron, *The Strange Voyage of Donald Crowhurst* (London: The Book Society 1970)

DAVID de LARA

DONALD CAMPBELL
300+ **A SPEED ODYSSEY**

HIS LIFE WITH BLUEBIRD

978 0 7509 7008 2

RRP £

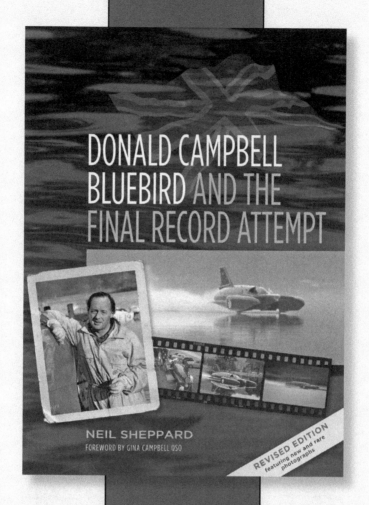

DONALD CAMPBELL BLUEBIRD AND THE FINAL RECORD ATTEMPT

NEIL SHEPPARD

FOREWORD BY GINA CAMPBELL QSO

REVISED EDITION
featuring new and rare
photographs

978 0 7524 8258 3

RRP £

DARING WOMEN OF HISTORY

AMELIA EARHART

MIKE ROUSSEL

978 0 7509 7948 1

RRP £

The destination for history
www.thehistorypress.co.uk